LARRY

CRABB'S

GOSPEL

LARRY
CRABB'S
GOSPEL

Martin & Deidre Bobgan
EastGate Publishers

Scripture quotations are taken from the Authorized
King James Version of the Holy Bible.

LARRY CRABB'S GOSPEL

Copyright © 1998 Martin and Deidre Bobgan
Published by EastGate Publishers
Santa Barbara, California

Library of Congress Catalog Card Number 98-93330
ISBN 0-941717-14-3

Printed in the United States of America

All scripture is given by inspiration of God, and is profitable for doctrine, for reproof, for correction, for instruction in righteousness:

That the man of God may be perfect, thoroughly furnished unto all good works.

(2 Timothy 3:16,17)

As ye have therefore received Christ Jesus the Lord, so walk ye in him:

Rooted and built up in him, and stablished in the faith, as ye have been taught, abounding therein with thanksgiving.

Beware lest any man spoil you through philosophy and vain deceit, after the tradition of men, after the rudiments of the world, and not after Christ.

For in him dwelleth all the fulness of the Godhead bodily.

(Colossians 2:6-9)

CONTENTS

Larry Crabb's Gospel

Dr. Lawrence Crabb, Jr. has written a number of books on counseling and Christian growth. From his background in psychology he comes to Scripture with a viewpoint that sounds both appealing and workable. He sees Christians struggling with difficult problems of living and wants to help. He also addresses serious problems having to do with superficiality and ineffective Christian living. He encourages people to develop a close relationship with God and to recognize their dependence on Him. Crabb's goals for a deeper walk with God, loving relationships, and effective Christian living have inspired many to follow his ideas and methods. However, the way he hopes to solve problems and lead people into a closer walk with the Lord depends heavily on psychological theories and techniques.

Crabb has been sensitive to the criticism of his work through the years. When people criticized him for using psychological terminology rather than biblical, he worked to improve his expression. Along the way he has discarded much of the psychological vocabulary while keeping the psychological concepts, but making them sound more biblical. When he discovered that aspects of his work did not fully satisfy and that he had not yet reached his goal of bringing the best of psychology and the Bible together for the entire body of Christ, he expanded his eclecticism.

Crabb's book *Connecting* (1997) includes some admissions, as do his other books. He gives the impression that

5

he is constantly discovering more about the very best way to help people change and grow in their relationship with God and with one another. Yet, his basic model of man and methodology of change remain firmly tied to the psychological theories presented in his earlier books. Each book has enough truth in it to make it appear that the most recent version of his approach is even better and more biblical than the previous one. He is careful, however, to justify the value of his previous work so that no one will misunderstand and think he has discarded his former ideas or repented of his former teachings.

Our first chapter in this book raises the question "Has Larry Crabb Changed?" Our next two chapters examine some of Crabb's additions and expansions developed in his later books. The remaining chapters are an abridged, revised, and updated version of "Inside-Out Theology," which was originally authored by Martin and Deidre Bobgan and Richard Palizay and was included as Part Two in our book *Prophets of PsychoHeresy I*. That section examined Crabb's works up through the publication of *Inside Out*. However, these chapters (four through ten) include additional examples and references from Crabb's later books. These references reveal that his original model is still intact even though he has expanded his eclecticism.

Crabb's amalgamation of psychology with the Bible impinges on the gospel message. Even his theologically correct statements feed into his psychotheology. For instance, he says,

> The gospel really is good news. When the internal troubles of people are exposed, when unsatisfied longings are felt in a way that leads to overwhelming pain, when self-centeredness is recognized in every fiber, then (**and not until then**) can the

wonder of the gospel be truly appreciated.[1]
(Emphasis added.)

While the first sentence is correct, the remainder of the
above quote adds psychological requirements beyond
those of Scripture.

Crabb interprets the message of the cross according to
his psychological ideas about the nature of man and how
he changes. The *gospel* becomes the good news that Jesus
meets the needs/longings/passions which motivate all
behavior from the unconscious. *Sin* becomes wrong
strategies for meeting the needs/longings/passions.
Confession is telling our stories and gaining insight into
those wrong strategies. *Full repentance* comes through
getting in touch with the pain of the past. Hence, the
gospel message itself is directly tied to a psychological
construct. Not only is the doctrine of man psychologized,
but the Father, Son, and Holy Spirit are made sub-
servient to Crabb's psychospiritual theories.

1

Has Larry Crabb Changed?

"Has Larry Crabb changed?" Has he moved away from integrating psychotherapeutic theories and techniques with the Bible? From the vantage point of having read Crabb's books over the past twenty years, we contend that Crabb has made some cosmetic changes, but they are not substantial. He has not discarded his confidence in psychotherapy and its underlying psychologies. Instead, he has expanded his eclecticism and his potential involvement in churches. This present volume answers the often-asked question, "Has Larry Crabb Changed?" and gives evidence to show that he continues to integrate psychotherapy and its underlying psychologies with the Bible.

Many people believed that Crabb's talk at the 1995 Moody Pastors' Conference and his 1995 *Christianity Today* interview, titled "Putting an End to Christian Psychology," signaled an about-face on psychology and Christian psychology. But, after reading and analyzing Crabb for years, we knew better. In a subsequent *Christianity Today* Letters to the Editor column, Crabb proved us right. The following is quoted from his letter to *Christianity Today* :

> I am neither crusading against psychology nor do I want to put an end to Christian psychology. . . .
> Positioning me as an antipsychology crusader who wants to end Christian psychology is badly inaccurate and places me in company where I don't belong. I am a friend of Christian counseling; I am not part of the antipsychology movement; and I am grateful for the many godly men and women who faithfully represent Christ in their professional counseling.[1]

In spite of the *Christianity Today* headlines, it is obvious that Crabb still supports his past books, his psychologized model of "biblical counseling," counseling for pay, and the unbiblical American Association of Christian Counselors. Moreover, it is doubtful that Crabb disagrees with any of the books he has written. While he may sound as if he disagrees with his former emphasis, he justifies its use in the same breath, as in the following statement from his 1997 book, *Connecting*.

> Before in my counseling, I spent too much time with the flesh. I over-studied doubt, denial, self-preserving psychological dynamics, and our selfishly driven strategies for relating to people. These topics are **worthy of serious investigation**, but it's easy

(and appealing to the flesh) to become more fasci-
nated with these matters than we need to be and, in
the process, less appreciative of the power available
in experiencing Christ.[2] (Bold added.)

But, where is the repentance? He says what he psychologically looked for in the powerful unconscious was
"worthy of serious investigation." But, now he has added
a new dimension to his psychological eclecticism. Following his secular counterparts, he is here searching the
depths to find goodness. He says:

> Looking back, I think I failed to emphasize that
> beneath all the bad is goodness, that a careful explo-
> ration of the redeemed heart does not sink us in a
> cesspool; it's more like mining for gold in a dirty
> cave.[3]

Crabb is still fossicking about in the unconscious, but
now he is looking for the "goodness" as well as the "doubt,
denial, self-preserving psychological dynamics, and our
selfishly driven strategies for relating to people." That
may be a shift, but it is not repentance. It is what eclectic
therapists tend to do to keep their therapy current.

"Moving the Couch into the Church"

Crabb's interest in the church's involvement in
personal ministry can be seen in his earliest books. His
first two books established him as one who looks to
psychology for answers to life's problems, attempts to
combine psychology with Christianity, and believes that
psychology should be brought into the local church. They
are titled *Basic Principles of Biblical Counseling* (1975)[4]
and *Effective Biblical Counseling* (1977).[5]

In describing Crabb's first book, *Basic Principles of Biblical Counseling*, the publisher says:

> This book is written out of the conviction that "the local church should and can successfully assume responsibility within its ranks for restoring troubled people to full, productive lives." Dr. Crabb has made a serious study of a biblically based approach to helping people who have emotional problems. "Koinonia" fellowship —**the practice of true community** —is an essential environment for healing and restoration.[6] (Bold added.)

Themes of a "biblically based approach to helping people" and "the practice of true community" are developed throughout his writings. However, Crabb's biblical approach includes a broad array of extra-biblical material drawn from the psychological theories of unsaved individuals.

"Moving the Couch into the Church" was an apt title for Crabb's article published twenty years ago in *Christianity Today* (September 22, 1978). In that article Crabb speaks about his prior view of *"psychological* problems and *spiritual* problems." He mentions how his "line of thinking received a gradual jolt."[7] The result of his "jolt" is that he "shifted" in his thinking. Crabb says, "And the answers I've come up with have impelled the most recent progression in my thinking."[8] This "gradual jolt," shift, and "recent progression" portrayed by Crabb in that article occurred over twenty years ago, but the jolt-shift-progression in thinking are the ways he has portrayed himself along the way.

In the same article, Crabb contends that "a personal relationship with Christ is a **necessary foundation** for dealing with all problems, psychological or spiritual."[9]

(Bold added.) Note his words *"necessary foundation."* After Crabb moved from "secular employment as a psychologist to enter private practice," he says that he:

> . . . experienced another shift in my thinking, not really a change but rather a natural progression in my belief that Christ is the **indispensable core** of effective personal adjustment.[10] (Bold added.)

Note the words *"indispensable core."* Crabb believes that "Christ is a necessary foundation" and "Christ is the indispensable core" for dealing with all problems. This theme of Christ being "necessary" and "indispensable" is consistent with Crabb over the past twenty years of writing. So, what is the problem with that? The problem is that Crabb has never said and does not believe that Christ is **sufficient** in that He is **enough**. In contrast to Crabb, we say nothing needs to be added. None of the psychological opinions of men that Crabb has been promoting over the years are needed along with Christ.

To dramatize this difference, which may seem small, but is actually huge, we ask a question related to each of Crabb's statements. Is "a personal relationship with Christ" a "necessary" or a **necessary and sufficient** "foundation for dealing with all problems, psychological or spiritual"? And, is Christ only "the indispensable core of effective personal adjustment" to which psychology is a necessary adjunct? Or is Christ "the indispensable [**whole**] of effective personal adjustment"? While these changes may appear minor, they express the intention of 2 Timothy 3:16-17:

> All scripture is given by inspiration of God, and is profitable for doctrine, for reproof, for correction, for instruction in righteousness: That the man of God

may be perfect, thoroughly furnished unto all good works.

These are changes to which Crabb and his followers will not subscribe. The difference is between a fully biblical position and a compromised one. Crabb's integration compromises both the intent of Scripture and the historic application of the Word to human living. But, there is no excuse for such compromise. The church did very well without psychology for almost 2000 years.

Crabb also says in his 1978 article:

> Effective biblical counseling requires encouragement, exhortation, and enlightenment. God intends the local church to provide these elements. Counseling therefore belongs ideally in the local church and not in the private professional office.[11]

We repeat Crabb's last sentence, "Counseling therefore belongs ideally in the local church and not in the private professional office." Note the words *counseling*, *ideally* and *not*. We would speak of "ministry," which Crabb labels "counseling"; we would say "solely" rather than "ideally"; and we would say "never" rather than "not." We would change his sentence to read: "[Ministry] therefore belongs [solely] in the local church and [never] in the private professional office," if "private professional office" refers to psychologically trained individuals selling their psychotherapeutic services to Christians. Here again is the difference between a compromised position and one that trusts fully in the Word of God and the work of the Holy Spirit.

Crabb further says in his 1978 article:

> Am I then hanging a "for rent" sign on my office
> door and moving into the pastor's study? No I don't
> consider private counseling *wrong*.[12] (Italics his.)

Crabb's words, "I don't consider private counseling
wrong," express the position he has continued to hold
over the past twenty years. Contrary to Crabb's position
and based upon extensive academic research alone, we
would state categorically that it is wrong for believers to
participate in this unproven practice, because they
already have the presence and the promises of God. They
can "come boldly unto the throne of grace, that we may
obtain mercy, and find grace to help in time of need"
(Hebrews 4:16). Even if such research did not exist, biblical reasons alone should discourage believers from
becoming involved in professional counseling, which
Crabb still strongly supports.

Our primary objection to the use of psychotherapy
and Christian psychology is not based merely on research
or on its confused state of self-contradiction or its phony
scientific facade. Our primary objection is not even based
on the attempts to explain human behavior through personal opinion presented as scientific theory. Our greatest
objection to psychotherapy and Christian psychology is
that, without proof or justification, it has compromised
the Word of God, the power of the cross, and the work of
the Holy Spirit among Christians.

Crabb explains his position regarding private counseling this way:

> I rather see [private counseling] as **less than the
> best**, something that exists and will probably
> continue to exist because churches are generally not
> doing a very good job of enlightening, exhorting, and
> encouraging. My concern is to help churches do a

better job so counseling can move into the local church where I think it belongs.[13] (Bold added.)

Note his expression, "less than the best." This statement sounds as if Crabb is wholeheartedly supporting a biblical care of souls centered around encouraging, exhorting, and enlightening and that "private counseling," meaning psychological counseling, will no longer be needed. However, that is NOT what Crabb is really saying. To discern what Crabb is saying, one must look into his proposal.

Crabb's Three Levels

Crabb proposes three levels of Christian counselors, based on his use of three words: *encouragement, exhortation*, and *enlightenment*. Crabb offers the following structure:

> Level I: "loving, supportive encouragement to their people who are struggling to live for God in a world opposed to him."

> Level II: "clear, practical exhortation to solve all conflicts in a manner consistent with Scripture."

> Level III: "sensitive, skilled enlightenment to replace foolish ideas about life with wisdom from God."[14]

Crabb describes Level III (Counseling by Enlightenment) as requiring a full-time position of expertise. He says:

> This counselor would **need to understand psychological functioning in some depth**: how

childhood experiences channel our thinking in wrong directions, where feelings come from, what controls behavior, how to unravel the tightly woven knots of foolish thinking, how to figure out the real causes behind surface problems, and so on.[15] (Bold added.)

In plain language, the person would have to be trained in the psychological theories of counseling. Such theories are not scientific theories but rather personal opinions developed by such people as Sigmund Freud, Carl Jung, Alfred Adler, Erich Fromm, Abraham Maslow, Carl Rogers, Albert Ellis and others.[16] One can readily see from this article and from his books that the help Crabb wants to give to churches comes from his training in the field of professional psychological counseling with its psychotherapeutic theories and methods.

Moving Psychology into the Church

Crabb's article "Moving the Couch into the Church" should have been titled "Moving Psychology into the Church." Crabb had not abandoned psychology when he wrote that article in which he proposes to drag psychology into the church. As we will demonstrate later, he has not yet abandoned psychology. He continues to attempt to drag it into the church where it does not belong, and he still sees the church as incapable of ministering effectively and successfully to believers without those certain insights he has gleaned from psychology. Crabb communicates volumes about how little confidence he has in the biblical care of souls, how much he believes that the Bible is insufficient to minister fully and completely to problems of living, and how unwilling he is to shut the door on psychology.

Crabb's attempts at integrating psychotherapy and its underlying psychologies with the Bible have encouraged a professionally based system that relies on the psychological wisdom of men, rather than a Christ-centered body of believers trusting in God and His Word. Crabb's encouragement to utilize the insights of psychology for the more difficult problems of living actually undermines the ordinary function of a body of believers with its appeal to and reliance on experts, such as himself, who have studied psychology and who can supposedly lead people into insight about their psyche's needs and strategies.

In proposing what he considers to be an ideal of believers ministering to one another according to the level of psychological expertise, Crabb actually strengthens the professional-centered system of therapy. His ideal of churches with professionally trained counselors on staff has come to reality in those many churches that now have a psychologically-trained professional counselor on staff. The more dependent Christians have become on such professional systems of "helps," the less they have had opportunities to exercise their own gifts of ministry and the less they have depended on Christ Himself.

Crabb's 1978 article also reveals his psychological basis for understanding problems of living. He says, "People came to me complaining of surface problems that I had to dig through to find the root difficulty."[17] In other writings before and after that article, Crabb reveals his confidence in and commitment to secular psychological understandings of man—to the undermining of the biblical truth about man.

We do not believe Crabb would disagree with what he wrote in his 1978 article. In fact, *Christianity Today* could rerun the article today and it would be as accurate a representation of Crabb now as it was then, except for a few changes in vocabulary, ways of expression, shifts in emphasis.

Crabb may change his terminology and expression. He may sound more biblical with each book, yet he has not disentangled himself from psychotherapeutic theories he likes. His book *Finding God* (1993) suggests that he has at last discovered the emptiness of psychotherapeutic theory.[18] But, once again he criticizes those aspects of psychotherapy he does not agree with and continues to belittle those who would depend on the Word of God and the work of the Holy Spirit in the believer. Just as in his earlier books, Crabb presents his seemingly right combination of psychology and Christianity. In *Finding God* Crabb attempts to help fellow believers come to know God better. However, once again he presents a murky mixture of worldly psychological notions with the Bible. Just as he gives a psychological means of sanctification in his books *Understanding People* and *Inside Out*, he presents a psychological process for finding God. His commitment to psychology continues on.

That is why the words "Larry Crabb's Antipsychology Crusade" on the cover of *Christianity Today* (1995) were so misleading. Readers were led into thinking Crabb was finally repenting of his psychologically-based "biblical counseling" model and his years of therapizing. The Crabb interview title "Putting an End to Christian Psychology" was also misleading.[19] Crabb was not on a crusade against professional therapy and integrating psychology and Christianity. No, as mentioned earlier in this chapter, Crabb submitted a Letter to the Editor to correct that impression. However, the words "Larry Crabb thinks therapy belongs back in the churches" were accurate and very reminiscent of Crabb's 1978 article which says:

I think that in the absence of organized malfunc-
tion, psychological problems stem from and are
maintained by inaccurate ideas about life (which
our sin nature warmly received), ineffective behavior patterns (which our sin nature argues are effective), and a lack of the sense of community (which
our sin nature seeks in all the wrong places). Therefore we need enlightenment to think right, exhortation to do right, and encouragement from a caring
community of fellow believers as we go about the
difficult business of living right.[20]

As mentioned earlier, Crabb in 1978 was proposing
three levels of counseling ministry: encouragement,
exhortation, and enlightenment, with enlightenment at
the top. By examining Crabb's books one can see that the
enlightenment to which he was referring is heavily
dependent on psychological theories devised by Sigmund
Freud, Alfred Adler, Albert Ellis, Abraham Maslow, and
Carl Rogers.

Crabb Changing His Doctrine?

Was Crabb changing his doctrine in 1995 or expanding his audience? In both the *Christianity Today* interview and in his talk at the 1995 Moody's Pastors'
Conference, Crabb shared what sounds like a new vision
for the church, but really echoes his 1978 article—to
equip the church to minister more effectively to help "people enter into a deeper, closer relationship with the
Lord."[23] This is indeed a lofty, admirable goal. But, how
does he, as a psychologist, propose to do that? He said he
does not know, but unless he clearly repudiates his earlier books and publicly repents of his model of man developed in *Understanding People*[21] and of processing people

as described in *Inside Out*,[22] one must assume that he will continue to use an integrationist approach as he attempts to move the couch into the church.

In his talk at Moody, Crabb said, "In our culture the work of individual shepherding has largely been turned over to the Christian Counseling Movement and that movement has professionalized shepherding into something that only vaguely resembles the Bible's idea of shepherding."[24] We agree with his concern that people choose psychotherapists over godly elders when they experience problems. However, there is no word of Crabb repenting from his own involvement in helping the church form that erroneous conclusion.

We also agree with Crabb's second major thesis of his talk at Moody:

> When you scratch deeply enough beneath the surface of people's problems, if there is no medical cause that appropriately requires expert medical help, then what you find beneath the surface of the kinds of problems that people bring to therapists like myself, what you find down deep inside the person is not what most counselors are trained to treat. You do not find, I suggest, a damaged self that needs repair by an expert of the self; you rather find **a troubled soul**, influenced by its three enemies – the world, the flesh, and the devil – someone who needs shepherding, not by an expert of the self, but by an elder of the soul.[25] (Bold added.)

To those words we say, "Amen." We have been saying the same thing for more than 25 years! However, we still must question **how he views the troubled soul**. His recent writings indicate that he has not abandoned his doctrine of the soul or his psychological doctrines of sanctification. He has not repudiated his ideas about the necessity of feeling the pain of the past before one can change his "current relational style," as developed in *Inside Out*. In that book he says:

> The first act of changing his current relational style had to be to open himself to feeling the pain of his past. Only then would he be in a position to realize how deeply determined he was to never feel that pain again. . . moving on to deeper levels of involvement with others required this man to more deeply feel his pain and to face his self-protective sin. The more deeply we enter our disappointment, the more thoroughly we can face our sin. **Unless we feel the pain of being victimized**, we will tend to limit the definition of our problem with sin to visible acts of transgression.[26] (Emphasis added.)

In his *Inside Out* Film Series, Crabb teaches that exposing the unconscious needs, fears, pains, and wrong strategies is a necessary means for personal Christian growth.[27] But, Scripture does not support such psychologically-driven requirements as having to feel the pain of being disappointed or victimized before the Holy Spirit can reveal the depths of our own sinfulness to us.

Crabb continues to teach those psychospiritual ideas even as he attempts to help "release a generation of elders" to fulfill their calling. He said in his talk at Moody:

> I want to help reverse the trend in evangelicalism of a growing dependence on counseling experts to deal with people's lives, a trend that is moving the church toward irrelevance, and to help develop a community of shepherds who know the sheep

entrusted to their care, and who deeply and powerfully engage with them.[28]

While Crabb wants to "help reverse the trend in evangeli-
calism of a growing dependence on counseling experts to
deal with people's lives," he would not say, as we do, that
we need to eliminate "counseling experts" altogether.

In that talk, Crabb said, "we must catch a vision of
what biblical eldering might look like in our culture."
Then he attempted to "develop a biblical framework." He
correctly referred to several passages having to do with
caring for God's flock. However, certain key words and
phrases reveal that Crabb has not moved away from psychotherapeutic notions—"profoundly listening to people's
stories," "identify deep struggles," "soul work," "deepest
longings."[29] Some of what he said in this talk has the
same flavor as *Inside Out*. For instance, in the Moody talk
he said:

> If the struggles reflect the troubled soul, a soul that
> is not aware of its calling, but resisting it, a soul
> that is not aware of its longings for Christ, but has
> cheapened them so it's satisfied with far less, a soul
> that hates itself and is not aware of its own unique-
> ness and what it can give to the body of Christ and
> therefore has no meaning and no reason to get up in
> the morning, if it's really a troubled soul that's
> beneath all these things we call psychological prob-
> lems—and I believe that it is—then we need elders,
> not experts.[30]

While Crabb wants to shift the work to the elders, his
doctrine of man and methodology of change remain
psychologically contaminated. As he teaches the elders
"to elder" Crabb may very well continue to say: "Until we
sense the deep discomfort we feel in relating as men and

women, we haven't touched the core of our struggle."[31]
He teaches the following in *Inside Out*:

> At the very center of our soul, we feel shame and
> fear that is attached to our identity as male or
> female. Males lack the healthy confidence that
> they're intact men who can move into their world
> unafraid of being completely destroyed by failure or
> disrespect. Females lack that quietly exhilarating
> awareness that they're secure women who can
> embrace their world with no worry of having their
> essential identity crushed by someone's abuse or
> rejection.[32]

His teachings about these feelings of shame relating
to doubts about ones sexual identity and "provide powerful motivation to protect ourselves from further wounds"
are still in place, as he says in *Inside Out*:

> *We will not face our self-protective maneuvering nor
> be passionately convicted about its sinfulness until
> we see its function is to preserve whatever is left of
> our identity as men and women.*[33] (Italics his).

The above quotes demonstrate Crabb's combination of
Freud's libido (sexual energy), Jung's animus and anima
(unconscious elements of masculinity and femininity),
and Maslow's hierarchy of needs.

Typical of those immersed in the psychotherapeutic
milieu, Crabb was open about his own personal struggles.
In attempting to demonstrate that he knows what it's like
to struggle deeply, he revealed shortcomings of others. He
confessed that, even while he was writing the book *The
Marriage Builder*,[34] his own marriage had died. In his
talk to the pastors at Moody Crabb said:

> When the marriage dies, there's no longer any affection left . . . my wife and I sat across from each other, looked at each other after our two boys were in bed and came to grips with what was happening in our marriage. Our marriage had died.[35]

While the intent may have been to confess his own failure in relationship, he also implied that his wife had also failed.

Later in the talk, while attempting to demonstrate his struggle and victory to reflect Christ to his son, Crabb revealed his son's failure. He said that one of his sons "was asked to leave a Christian university school where my books were used as texts." The reason for the dismissal was serious enough for Crabb to say, "My boy was asked to leave and had I been Dean, I would have asked him to leave."

Revealing the sins of others in order to be open and transparent in our psychological society and psychotainted churches flies in the face of real love as expressed in 1 Peter 4:8, "And above all things have fervent charity among yourselves: for charity shall cover the multitude of sins.."

One of our concerns about Crabb's model of counseling has to do with implementing a psychotherapeutic openness about one's personal life, past and present, that not only reveals the sins of others, but magnifies them.

Crabb's Pro-psychology Admission

Crabb continues to give great credence to those who practice psychotherapy, even while he recognizes the part therapists have played in undermining the work of elders. His Moody talk included the following admission:

As an active member of the Christian Counseling Movement for the past 25 years, I'm beginning to wonder if in the middle of the considerable good that I think we have done—and I'm not anti-counseling, **I'm not anti-professional counseling at all**, I think a lot of good has been done by godly Christian counselors, don't misunderstand me— but I **wonder** if in the middle of the considerable good that godly Christian counselors who operate in the professional setting have done, if perhaps without knowing it, certainly without intending it, if we have unwittingly helped to weave into the fabric of evangelical Christianity a very bad idea—an idea that has strengthened our dependence on counseling experts while weakening our confidence in what godly elders could do if encouraged and released to honor their calling.[36] (Bold added.)

We don't "wonder" as Crabb does; we know that Crabb and his Christian counselor friends have woven "into the fabric of evangelical Christianity a very bad idea." Crabb and his fellow Christian counselors have strengthened "dependence on counseling experts while weakening confidence" in God's Word, God's promises, God's Son, God's Spirit, and God's people. Without true repentance for over 20 years of such activity there is little hope for substantial change in Crabb.

Towards the end of his talk Crabb referred to when he had a full-time counseling practice and said:

And I believe in that context, I did some real good, and I believe those who love the Lord and are in that context now many times are doing real good – don't misunderstand me. **I believe it's an honor-**

able way to make a living. . . . Many committed Christian people are serving the Lord well in a counseling practice and if you or your people are finding help in **that setting**, my advice is praise God and **keep going**.[37] (Bold added.)

No, Crabb is **not** antipsychology. He is **not** opposed to psychological counseling. He is **not** "putting an end to Christian psychology." However, in contrast to what Crabb said, we have said and documented, both from the Bible and research literature, that psychological counseling is a dishonorable way to make a living. Also, "that setting" is an unbiblical one for a Christian to be in. Instead of advising, as Crabb does, to "keep going," we have demonstrated biblically and academically why Christians should get out.[38]

While Crabb is beginning to sense some of the things some of us have been saying for years, he has not repudiated his past and continues to inject psychology into his teachings. Crabb is still speaking out of both sides of his mouth. He speaks some of the same things some of us have been saying out of the right side of his mouth, but he continues some of the same psychogarble out of the other side. If he had a straight message, he would be apologizing for the balance of his life for all the havoc he and other psychologists have caused in the church. We have yet to hear him confess and repent of the serious errors of his unbiblical teachings. Instead, he adjusts his language to fit his next goal: training elders to elder. From what Crabb said at the Moody conference, it sounds as if he will continue the same processing of reliving painful disappointments.

Indications of Real Change

What might be indications of real change? If Crabb were to disagree with what he has formerly written, the honest thing for him to do would be to repudiate those writings publicly, let Christians know where he has been wrong, and request that his publishers discontinue printing any books that would be contrary to his present position. However, we do not believe Crabb will do this because there has been a consistent dependence on psychology and a high regard for professional psychological theories, methods, training, and therapy. And, there has been a consistent effort to move the couch into the church and to help Christians by means of the psychological wisdom of men along with the Word of God.

Because of his position on psychotherapy and its underlying psychologies, Crabb is guilty of what we call *psychoheresy*. We coined the term *psychoheresy* and gave it the following definition: a psychological heresy, a heresy because it is a departure from the Word of God and from the fundamental truth of the Gospel, a psychological heresy because the departure is the use of and support of unproven and unscientific psychological opinions of men instead of absolute confidence in the biblical truth of God. In spite of his various shifts throughout the past twenty years, Crabb continues to hold the door wide open to the integration of secular psychological counseling theories and therapies with the Bible.

While he currently decries the church's over-dependence on professional counselors, Crabb carries much of the responsibility for the church's acceptance and deepening dependence on psychotherapy and its underlying psychologies. The psychological way has been embraced by numerous Christian schools, seminaries, churches, missionary organizations, books, radio and other media, to the degree that many Christians assume that such psychological ideas are true and even biblical. With Crabb's popularity, the tentacles of the psychological way continue to strangle the thinking of many Christians.

What would be evidence of a real change on Crabb's part?

1. He would be anti-psychotherapy and its underlying psychologies.

2. He would confess and repent publicly for all his past promotion of psychology.

3. He would recommend that Christians not pay any attention to his past writings if they have copies of his books.

4. He would specifically indicate with which of his past writings and books he now disagrees.

5. He would ask the publishers of those books to place them out of print.

6. He would warn Christians about the dangers that exist in much of what is called "Christian psychology."

7. He would name those Christians and Christian organizations with whom he disagrees.

We know how painful it is to repent publicly of past writings and to ask a publisher to cease publishing a book. We've been there—done that. When we left the biblical counseling movement and wrote *Against "Biblical Counseling"—For the Bible* we asked Moody Press to discontinue offering our book *How to Counsel from Scripture*. They complied and put it out of print just when it appeared to be growing in popularity. Following the publishing of *Against "Biblical Counseling"—For the Bible*, we wrote a number of articles confessing our errors and retracting a number of former recommendations. We believe that Crabb would be just as forthright and do the same if he disagreed with his former writings. The fact that he has not is a tangible testimony that no real change has occurred.

2

Crabb's Shifts and Expansions

Larry Crabb's later books show a movement and shift in the direction of the church as being a community for Christian growth and maturity. In these books he emphasizes the possibility of powerful Christians effectively ministering in the context of the church. Some readers think the direction and emphasis of his later books indicate real change on Crabb's part, but instead it reveals Crabb's shifts and expansions. Crabb says in his 1996 book, *Hope When You're Hurting*, "The direction my mind is now taking fits comfortably with the slogan I attached to my ministry twenty years ago: 'Meeting counseling needs through the local church.'"[1] This book represents only a superficial change in Crabb's views, a little change of vocabulary here and a little change of expression there, but not a change in the essence of what he has taught through the years. Crabb's dream of transforming the church into a community is actually a continuation and expansion of his earlier ideas.

In 1997 Word Publishing published Larry Crabb's book *Connecting*. In that book Crabb says:

> In recent days, I have made a shift. I am now working toward the day when communities of God's people, ordinary Christians whose lives regularly intersect, will accomplish most of the good that we now depend on mental health professionals to provide. And they will do it by *connecting* with each other in ways that only the gospel makes possible.[2]

Crabb refers to a "shift," but there is no substantive change in his position from over twenty years ago, including his doctrine about a powerful unconscious with contents that need to be exposed if a person is to grow in his relationship with God, himself, and others.[3] As he said, only one year earlier, his current position "fits comfortably with the slogan I attached to my ministry twenty years ago." In *Connecting*, Crabb offers some conclusions:

> Beneath what our culture calls psychological disorder is a soul crying out for what only community can provide.[4]

> We must do something other than train professional experts to fix damaged psyches.[5]

He says accurately, "the conclusions don't feel entirely new, just more central."[6]

Note Crabb's sentence, "I am now working toward the day when communities of God's people, ordinary Christians whose lives regularly intersect, will accomplish most of the good that we now depend on mental health professionals to provide." Especially note the word *most*. Crabb says "most" because he still has faith in the psychological way, rather than full trust in God's Word empowered by the Holy Spirit to transform lives completely without the use of psychotherapy and its underlying psychologies. His use of the word *most* does not necessarily indicate that he believes ordinary Christians can do much more than he thought they could twenty years ago. Instead, the population seeking counseling in the church has exploded with more people wanting counseling for less serious problems. Moreover, Crabb has clearly taught that all Christians need to become aware of their unconscious needs, pain and strategies in order to become rightly dependent on God. In other words, all believers need the kind of psychospiritual processing for exposure, awareness, and change that he has espoused throughout his books.

As Crabb taught twenty years earlier, Christians can deal with less complex problems with Level I (encouragement) and Level II (exhortation) counselors; but the more complex problems require a Level III counselor who "would need to understand psychological functioning in some depth."[7] Without doing away with the first three levels, Crabb has added another level in his later books. Now he is looking for powerful people who not only meet the qualifications of Levels I, II, and III, but are so powerful that they can release the good in a person as well as expose the bad. These powerful people could be professional counselors or even elders in the church.[8]

Regarding his twenty-five years of counseling, Crabb says in *Connecting*, "I look back on all that time with great satisfaction. By any standard, I have enjoyed success in my professional career and have helped some folks along the way."[9] Does that sound like regret for his professional practice or the professional training of others? Not at all. He speaks of "satisfaction" and "success." No apologies. No regrets. No repentance. And, no requesting publishers of his past books to discontinue offering them because he has changed his mind.

Through the years Crabb has presented his counseling model as "biblical" and has worked to "move the couch into the church." He describes himself having served as a "professional therapist and trainer of counselors,"[10] but now having a dream to train elders and shepherds to elder and to shepherd God's flock within the context of the church. He is thus extending his psychospiritual mixture of theories and practices into the heart of the church.

Crabb contends that Christians turn to psychologically trained counselors because the church has not functioned as a mutually healing community. He considers one reason to be that "Protestants have tended to devalue and mostly abandon the practice of formal confession."[11] Crabb thus encourages pastors and elders to help people tell their stories in such a way as to expose the contents of the unconscious, become aware of their deepest hidden pain and fear, and confess the strategies they contrived to deny the pain.

Crabb's contention that the church is not ministering to people with problems of living is partly right. However, one major reason why the church has failed to minister to those suffering from problems of living is that pastors and parishioners have succumbed to the intimidation put forth by mental health organizations, secular psychotherapists, and professional Christian counselors, including Crabb. The mental health industry made an all-out effort during the 1960s to intimidate pastors with the idea that pastors were inadequate in dealing with psychological problems. If pastors were inadequate the assumption was that ordinary Christians could not help either. Thus most shepherds and the sheep learned to refer problem-laden people out to professional counselors. Other shepherds and sheep became psychologically trained themselves.

With such intimidation, most Christians are afraid to minister unless they are trained in psychology. Along with this intimidation came a whole host of programs to promote and dispense psychotherapeutic theories and techniques, including books, radio programs, and seminars. The failure of the church does not lie in the inability of ordinary Christians being able to minister to one another in the body of Christ through Christ's indwelling presence, but rather in the lies it believes about helping people with problems.

Due to the vast amount of intimidation in which Crabb has held an active role, the church has failed to minister as fully as it can. Yet it is still far more successful at dealing with problems of living than psychotherapists. Just think of how much the church could minister if the intimidation were removed or if people truly turned back to the Word of God and trusted Him in ministering to one another in the body of Christ. This would require a real turn-about, however, because of the vast trust already laid at the feet of psychotherapy and its underlying psychologies. We say this because such psychological ideas have so infested sermons, seminaries, Bible colleges, books, and so-called Christian media that even Christians untrained in psychology may inadvertently minister a psychospiritual mixture. That is why we urge believers to do as the Bereans who "searched the scriptures daily, whether those things were so" (Acts 17:11).

Crabb does admit that psychotherapists are limited in what they can do. But he still recommends them. For years we have pointed out that psychotherapists use only their ears to hear and their mouths to speak, but almost never use their hands (except to receive cash, check or credit card) or feet (unless it's to run after those who don't pay) to help, particularly outside the office setting. We have contended that no therapy or therapist's conversation can compete with the work of the church. Thus we agree with Crabb that ministry should be in the church, but we oppose psychologically tainted programs that, while appearing to equip, will further intimidate many believers from being involved in mutual care and will blunt the true power of the Word.

In spite of his admission that therapists are limited in what they do, Crabb says:

> I have often said that if one of my sons, who are both happily married, got into some significant marital struggle and wanted help outside their own efforts to heal things, I could recommend to each of them a good professional counselor in their area.[12]

Crabb stands divided. After generally criticizing elders for not shepherding the sheep, he says:

> Certainly some elders meaningfully shepherd and, regrettably, some Christian counselors do little that could be called Christlike shepherding. But after twenty-five years as a professional therapist and trainer of counselors for fourteen, I have concluded that **more shepherding goes on in counseling offices than in churches**. And yet when a good professional biblical counselor counsels, he or she is coming closer to what the Bible means by shepherding than by what our culture understands to be expert professional treatment. But shepherding

properly belongs to the church community.[13] (Bold added.)

That is a clear statement of Crabb's confidence in the ability of psychologically trained professionals to shepherd and disciple God's sheep and of his apparent blindness to the fact that believers in their mutual care of souls already accomplish more true shepherding than any psychological counselor can offer. His reference to biblical counselors in the above quote would refer to those who are integrationists, since he calls his integration "biblical counseling" and because he is highly critical of those who refuse to integrate psychology in their personal ministry.

Psychology or the Bible?

Because Crabb criticizes some aspects of psychology and assures his readers that he biblically screens all material from psychology before he uses it, many have **assumed** that his model of counseling is biblical. And, now that he is wanting to encourage and equip elders and shepherds to do an even greater work than counseling, his readers continue to assume that his ideas for helping people are biblical, when in fact they are made up of a combination of psychology and Christianity.

His attempt to use the Bible to screen only the best from psychological counseling systems illustrates the fact that one cannot remain true to the Word of God while mixing it with the unproven, unscientific psychological wisdom of men. He even recognizes inherent dangers in integration as he warns:

In spite of the best of intentions to remain biblical, it is frighteningly easy to admit concepts into our thinking which compromise biblical content.

> Because psychologists have spent up to nine years studying psychology in school and are pressed to spend much of their reading time in their field in order to stay current, it is inevitable that we develop a certain "mind set." **The all-too-common but disastrous result is that we tend to look at Scripture through the eyeglasses of psychology when the critical need is to look at psychology through the glasses of Scripture.**[14] (Bold added.)

Yet, in spite of his own recognition of danger and his sincere effort to remain biblical, Crabb's interpretation of Scripture has come "through the eyeglasses of psychology." If he had truly looked "at psychology through the glasses of Scripture," he would have turned away from the myths of psychology and back to the Word of God as the **sufficient** means of understanding people and helping them change and grow. Nevertheless, he remains staunch in his resistance to those who would rely solely on the Word of God and the work of the Holy Spirit as ministered in the body of Christ.

Integrationists such as Larry Crabb distort the position of those of us who oppose psychotherapy and its underlying psychologies. Integrationists contend that those who are against mixing the models and methods of psychotherapy with the Bible do not believe that true Christians suffer from deep emotional feelings or valleys of despair. Such integrationists fail to comprehend that the Lord and His Word are sufficient to minister to the depths of despair and problems of living having to do with loneliness and depression. For instance, in his book *Finding God*, Crabb says:

One school of thought tells us that feeling hurt and longing to feel better is selfish. Students in this school warn against preoccupation with self and the corrupting influence of psychology. They insist that trying to understand our thirst-driven passions and desires is an ungodly concession to "pagan" psychology. They further declare that healing personal wounds and restoring a sense of enjoyable identity is rubbish—dangerous, humanistic rubbish.[15]

Crabb's statement implies that the Bible-without-psychology "school of thought tells" people that one must deny feelings and never want to feel better in order to be unselfish. Feeling hurt is a natural response to many of life's adversities. However, feeling hurt may also be sinfully intensified through the kind of introspective psychotherapy promoted by Crabb's books. Selfishness can certainly motivate "feeling hurt and longing to feel better," but it is only one of many possibilities.

Crabb's next sentence, "Students in this school warn against preoccupation with self and the corrupting influence of psychology." This is accurate. The Bible does not teach us to be preoccupied with ourselves, but rather with Christ and with one another. That does not mean that one must pretend feelings are not there, but that God calls believers to turn to Him, rather than to the ungodly wisdom of such men as Freud, Adler, Maslow, and the other psychotherapeutic theorists to whom Crabb is indebted. Jesus said,

> Come unto me, all ye that labour and are heavy laden, and I will give you rest. Take my yoke upon you, and learn of me; for I am meek and lowly in heart: and ye shall find rest unto your souls. For my

yoke is easy, and my burden is light. (Matthew 11:28-30.)

Crabb's next sentence in the above quotation from *Finding God* is misleading: "They insist that trying to understand our thirst-driven passions and desires is an ungodly concession to 'pagan' psychology." Dealing biblically with passions and desires is what is needed. But, "trying to understand our thirst-driven passions and desires" with the psychological wisdom of men presented throughout Crabb's books **is** "an ungodly concession to 'pagan' psychology."

One may gain a true biblical understanding of one's passions and desire from Scripture. In fact, the only accurate understanding of oneself comes from God. He is the only one who truly understands us and His Holy Spirit together with His Word reveals us to ourselves. Our objection is to using ungodly psychology to do what only God and His Word can do. The kind of psychology used by Crabb and other integrationists may appear to approximate reality, but these psychological theories are made of whole cloth out of the imagination and subjective experience of the theorist.[16] Thus people are led away from true self-knowledge and into self-serving theories that de-emphasize sin and intensify self-preoccupation even while attempting to move a person from self to altruism.

Crabb's final sentence from the above quote is: "They further declare that healing personal wounds and restoring a sense of enjoyable identity is rubbish—dangerous, humanistic rubbish." Such a statement makes it sound as though those who are anti-psychology want people to suffer and be miserable. Just the opposite is true. However, much of what is identified as "personal wounds" that need healing are in fact sinful responses to circumstances. Jesus does indeed bring repentance, restoration, and healing, but He does so through revealing Himself to the sinner and the sinner to himself, rather than through the various psychological methods devised by unbelievers and promoted by professing Christians. The Bible is clear about the identity of a Christian: child of God, temple of the Holy Spirit, a vital member of the body of Christ. Is there any identity more enjoyable both now and for eternity? Furthermore, Paul's declaration of identity applies to all true Christians:

> I am crucified with Christ: nevertheless I live; yet not I, but Christ liveth in me: and the life which I now live in the flesh I live by the faith of the Son of God, who loved me, and gave himself for me. (Galatians 2:20.)

We contend that integrating psychology with Christianity for the purpose of counseling or shepherding robs the Christian of the best God has for him.

Up-to-Date Eclecticism

Twenty years prior Crabb said, "I had to dig through to find the root difficulty."[17] Throughout twenty years of writing Crabb has held onto his integration position and his view of the unconscious. In *Connecting* he says:

> I want to be honest about the insecurities, fears, and inadequacies that lie hidden in our hearts beneath the appearances we may present to others. I want us to speak with neither shame nor pride about the dark nights of our soul. . . but I do want us to look beneath all that is difficult. . . .[18]

While most readers will probably not connect these current comments to past writings, those of us who have read Crabb over the years see that he is still espousing an eclectic psychospiritual model much the same as at the beginning. In keeping with his secular counterparts, Crabb has adjusted his eclectic model to fit the times. We see the same eclecticism expressed over and over again through the years in his various books. The main differences are in vocabulary, expression and current emphasis, but his psychospiritual model, while sounding more spiritual, is still contaminated with ungodly psychological roots.

The following two statements by Crabb express his current expansion:

> I want us to see that he has placed powerful urges to do good in the deepest recesses of our regenerated hearts. That's what the New Covenant is all about. Something wonderful and beautiful and resilient is within us that no abuse, rejection, or failure can ever destroy. I want us to focus on that![19]
>
> . . . .
>
> I want us to relate to one another, not as a moralist to sinner or therapist to patient, but as saint to saint, father to child, friend to friend, as true lovers, with the confidence that we can help each other believe that, by the grace of God, there is something good beneath the mess.[20]

As usual with Crabb, something beneath the surface must be brought to the surface. Crabb's emphasis on looking for hidden treasure may make people feel accepted by God and others and make people feel better about themselves, but not necessarily better about God. The shift easily deteriorates into people thinking more highly about themselves, at least about their so-called hidden goodness.

These two statements also reveal how up-to-date Crabb is as a psychologist. *The Family Therapy Networker*, a professional psychotherapy journal, reports new trends in therapy:

> The last decade has seen a fundamental shift in the way many clinicians regard their therapeutic role. Rather than being exorcists casting out hidden traumas and deficits, therapists these days look more like treasure hunters seeking the unrecognized gems in their clients' lives and personalities.[21]

Concepts of pathology and deficit are being replaced with concepts of resilience, competence, and client empowerment. The article further reports:

> Clinicians have discovered that clients seem to improve most easily when they are encouraged to **plumb for the best** in their own natures and **dig deep into the untapped reservoirs of valor, determination, intelligence, optimism, faith, love, friendship and discipline** that ultimately can heal them.[22] (Bold added.)

While this approach to therapy may seem to be an improvement over some of the therapies that are going out of vogue, psychotherapy remains culture-bound. Jerome Frank remarks, "A historical overview of Western psychotherapy reveals that the dominant psychotherapeutic approach of an era reflects contemporary cultural attitudes and values."[23] What is in vogue reflects the current cultural preferences. In contrast, Jesus Christ is the same yesterday, today, and forever, and the Word of God is eternal.

The following illustrates how Crabb has incorporated this psychological trend into his own eclecticism without losing the major aspects of his former psychological explanations about the nature of man. In his section of *Hope When You're Hurting*, Crabb describes a man by the name of Steve who has a problem with anger. He connects this present anger with what he sees as Steve's damaging background, but then says:

> But understanding all the subtle forces that have combined to damage Steve's sense of masculine identity may not be necessary.[24]

Crabb has already come to a psychological conclusion, that "Steve's sense of masculine identity" has been damaged. While he says that a psychodynamic understanding "may not be necessary," he does not declare that a psychodynamic understanding is **not** necessary. He does not close the door to psychology. He has already established a partial psychological diagnosis, and the prescription for what the church might do is not free of psychotherapeutic dynamics. He says that if such "understanding of all the subtle forces" were necessary, one would need "psychodynamic experts," but:

> If not, if unreleased love due to **unembraced hunger and unacknowledged selfishness (with a denial of its impact)** is the problem, then godly Christians who can discern the hunger and selfishness in the soul will be able to powerfully encourage the release of Steve's love toward Gloria [his wife].[25] (Bold added.)

What Crabb expects Christians to do is to see inside another person in a manner very similar to the way a psychodynamic therapist might attempt to see. Once again it is the unconscious needs for security and significance recast as "unembraced hunger" and selfish strategies recast as "unacknowledged selfishness (with a denial of its impact)" that prevent what Crabb believes to be the release of good passions that lie trapped below the surface.

Besides continuing an eclectic combination of psychological theories and therapies, Crabb assumes that if people have discernment they can see inside another person. But, who "can discern the hunger and selfishness in the soul" of another person? What mere mortal might have the audacity to believe he can discern the hidden thoughts and intents of another person's heart? Scripture declares this to be the work of the Word and the Holy Spirit (e.g., Heb. 4:12,13). Those who seek to look into another person's soul, analyze it, and change the person from the inside out and those who specialize in identifying the idols of the heart have had to dip into the psychological theories of the world. The Bible clearly identifies sin, and the Holy Spirit reveals the idols of one's own heart. However, the Bible does **not** instruct anyone to look into another person's soul to identify, analyze, or release the contents. One must go outside Scripture to do what the Bible does not teach.

Supposing that one person, whether a "psychodynamic expert" or an ordinary Christian trained in Crabb's techniques of discerning, exposing, and releasing, can look into the soul of another smacks of both arrogance and naiveté. The Lord gives many opportunities to open people's eyes and He is fully able to do so. When the Word of God is read or preached and heard, the Holy Spirit has

ample opportunity to open a person's eyes to sinful attitudes, thoughts, and actions.

Ministry to one another in the body of Christ is the
normal outworking of the Christian life. It is how the
body functions. However, Crabb is adding a psychodynamic dimension of discerning another person's thoughts
and intents of the heart that the Word does not support.
Here is how Crabb suggests how powerful Christians can
pour themselves into fellow believers. They must be able
to know the nature and contents of the hidden region of
another person's soul. They are to listen in such a way as
to attribute worth to the other person (appealing to what
Crabb has earlier identified as a person's deepest need)
and then look inside that person. Crabb explains:

> The actual process of pouring would include *pro-
> found listening*, the kind of sustained attention that
> we give only to what we deeply value. When men
> and women feel valued and meaningfully honored,
> something stirs within them that longs to be worthy
> of that respect. Pouring also includes *sensitive dis-
> cernment*. A godly Christian could gently expose the
> selfishness of Steve's commitment to never hurt
> again like he did with his mother by helping him see
> the pain he is causing his wife today.[26]

This description is dependent on Crabb's psychological understanding described in his book *Understanding
People*. The method is once again being able to see into
the hidden region of the soul (the psyche) of another and
then exposing it's powerful motivating contents.

What seems to be an added dimension to Crabb's
approach is actually a greater emphasis on his 1978 article, "Moving the Couch into the Church," and releasing
the goodness. In *Hope When You're Hurting*, he says:

If Steve's heart has already been changed by the gospel, the awareness of the damage he is causing will awaken a deeper desire to bless Gloria. As that longing surfaces [from beneath the waterline of the unconscious], the godly Christian [trained in Crabb's psychospiritual dynamics of digging, exposing, and releasing] could further pour into Steve's life by sharing what happens in his (the older Christian's) heart as he sees Steve's longing to give to Gloria.[27]

Here is the psychologically-bound connection of sharing that Crabb develops further in his book *Connecting*, in which he encourages the church to be a community with powerful people who are powerfully able to minister to the hidden needs of people.

Releasing Hidden Gems

In *Connecting* he continues with the idea of releasing the hidden gems. Crabb now is searching the depths for people's goodness and releasing that goodness. He proposes how God releases the goodness:

First, he provides us a taste of Christ delighting in us—*the essence of connection.*
° Accepting who we are
° Envisioning who we could be

Second, he diligently searches within us for the good he has put there—*an affirming exposure*:
° Remaining calm when badness is visible
° Keeping confidence that goodness lies beneath

> Third, he engagingly exposes what is bad and
> painful—*a disruptive exposure*
> ° Claiming the special opportunities to reveal grace
> that the difficult content of our hearts provide. [28]
> (Italics his.)

Note here that this is not God acting directly through
His Word or His Spirit, but through Crabb's psychological
means of exposure in a safe environment. Crabb still
wants to expose what is in the depths of a hidden region
of the person (in a motivating unconscious that influences
and may even determine behavior), but now he wants to
expose some good along with some bad, all of which lies
hidden outside the person's consciousness. The exposure
is a man-made methodology.

While he is still in the business of exposing the
badness, he expands the exposure to include the goodness. He says:

> But we spend too much time exploring our badness,
> dwelling on our pain, and understanding the dark-
> ness within us in hopes of weakening our unruly
> passions. Or we disregard the mess as nothing but
> an opportunity for excuse making and exhort people
> to live up to good standings. Neither approach prop-
> erly takes into account the state of affairs brought
> about by the New Covenant.[29]

It isn't that he wants to give up all that exploration.
He wants to look for what he calls the "good urges" that
he believes are hidden beneath the surface along with the
"bad urges," and he believes that there is "power waiting
to be released" as people establish connection through
"profound acceptance."[30] But more than that he says:

If, however, the connection goes beyond acceptance to include penetrating wisdom and spiritual discernment, then friendship has deepened into shepherding. Shepherds not only jump up and down at the sight of another, they also spot the Spirit's bright work in the darkest recesses of a regenerate soul.[31]

Thus we have the perfect Rogerian environment of acceptance, the "penetrating wisdom and spiritual discernment" of depth psychology, and the new psychological trend of identifying a person's positive attributes. One might object to this psychological description of the above quote, but as long as Crabb does not repent openly and directly for mixing the psychologies underlying psychotherapy in all of his former books, one is left with a psychological interpretation of such statements. In addition, he hangs on to enough of the psychological techniques in his later books to demonstrate that he is still an integrationist who picks and chooses what psychological ideas to add to the Bible.

Crabb gives a personal example of how something good can be released through another. After recalling how his fifth-grade teacher, Mr. Erb, said to him: "I've noticed you like words. I've been thinking about that. Larry, one day you could be a writer." Crabb says:

Mr. Erb's comment . . . released something. His words sounded strangely familiar, like the echo of a sentence I had heard before. They reached something in me that was already there.[32]

The truth is I think I *had* heard those words before. Is it possible that, from my earliest days, the Holy Spirit had been breathing that same thought into my soul, whispering it to me even in my mother's womb?[33]

This highly speculative statement presents additional concerns about Crabb's ideas about the human condition and his imagination about the Holy Spirit's supposed communication with him in his mother's womb.

Crabb proposes the powerful kind of person one must be to really help people:

> We need more than people who will enter our battles and give us a vision of what Christ will do. We need folks who can talk to us wisely and sensitively and meaningfully about our deepest battles, our most painful memories, and our secret sins. My contention, however, is that the person best qualified to engage with us at those levels is the person most filled with the energy of Christ. That person may or may not be a trained professional. The energy that fills a truly qualified helper includes far more than "mere" compassion, it involves engagement that goes miles beyond listening skills; it offers **probing wisdom** and life-giving words that provide more than the promise to pray, gestures of support, and bits of advice.[34] (Bold added.)

Once again the person must dig with "probing wisdom" into the hidden region, expose the pain and sinful strategies for avoiding the pain, and have a vision for what gems lie hidden waiting to be recognized and released. While Crabb admits, "That person may or may not be a trained professional," he does say, "Of course we need training."[35] He says:

> I envision a training program to help people speak with the wise, informed energy of Christ that includes charts, lectures, books, supervision, and critique. I want people to have some reasonable clue

about where to move when someone admits a loss of interest in life.[36]

Thus we see Crabb's expanded vision to bring his updated eclectic, integrated model of man and methodology of change into the churches. While Crabb may decry the way people want explanations and formulas and criticize those who provide them, he himself has provided numerous explanations and formulas. Even though his later books do not sound as formulized, he continues to explain the human condition with a mixture of psychology and Christianity and he continues to present steps to follow. He has not yet said that his explanations and formulas have led people in the wrong direction. The most he says is that there's more to finding God and connecting than explanations and formulas.

Still, he is hoping to guide people into finding God and connecting with powerful people in such a way as to reveal their capacities for goodness. Since he still hangs onto a psychospiritual understanding of the nature of man and means of sanctification, and since he still supports the practice of psychotherapy, Crabb continues to be part of the problem about which he expresses concern.

Rather than discarding a psychological sanctification, he is making it more available to Christians within the church and adding a dimension of psychospiritual connection. While Crabb is personally moving in the direction of equipping the church with his ideas, he still supports the practice of psychological therapy. Even in his goal to establish "connecting" in the church he mixes ideas and practices from the field of psychotherapy with his understanding of Scripture.

Crabb's Commitment to Professional Counseling

In Appendix A of *Connecting,* Crabb says, "The talking cure does not belong only to professionals."[37] Note the word *only*. We would have left that word out altogether. For Christians we would say, "The talking cure does not belong to [psychologically trained] professionals." If Crabb had truly changed, he would say the same. Crabb has always allowed for churches to do **some** of the work with problems of living and usually the simple ones at that. The only change Crabb has made is to somewhat expand the amount of ministry believers can do in helping one another. This is a timely expansion because of the increasing numbers of people who are seeking help for less serious problems of living. Furthermore, Crabb is expanding the numbers of people needing his brand of "talking cure" to include every Christian interested in spiritual growth.

But has Crabb repudiated counseling psychology and particularly "Christian psychology" as we did in our book *The End of "Christian Psychology"*? Absolutely not! Has Crabb stated clearly, as we have in *Competent to Minister: The Biblical Care of Souls*, that believers are fully competent to minister without the aid of psychology or without being referred to psychotherapists? Absolutely not!

In Appendix B of *Connecting*, Crabb asks, "Is there a place for the counseling professional?" He answers, "Concerns that are best understood by empirical research are best handled by a qualified professional."[38] The problem with that statement is that empirical research can be used to understand such activities as ESP, biorhythms, fingertip reading, and psychic phenomena. Empirical research has been used to understand everything from art to Zen and from prayer to politics. Crabb's statement opens a Pandora's box of possibilities.

Crabb then says:

> Empirically researchable concerns do not fundamentally reflect struggles in the souls, rather they follow relatively predictable patterns in terms of cause, nature, and resolution. They should therefore be treated by trained people who are substantially familiar with these elements and skilled in applying what they know.[39]

Crabb confuses the subject of professional talk therapy with biological, medical, educational and vocational issues. Into this morass he throws ADHD (Attention Deficit Hyperactivity Disorder), antisocial behavior, "marital communication patterns and handling teen rebellion."[40]

He presents the following question in Appendix B: "Are you saying that professional counselors are not necessary for handling personal problems growing out of soul struggles?"[41] Here is a perfect question phrased by Crabb himself that he should be able to answer directly and simply, but what is his answer? He answers, "Theoretically, yes." We would say, "Emphatically, yes!" He equivocates by saying, "As long as the resources of community [church] remain undeveloped, professional counselors will occupy a legitimate place."[42]

In contrast we would say unequivocally that professional counselors **never** occupy a legitimate place for the Christian. The very presence of the open door to professional psychotherapy stands as an intimidation and an invitation for churches to refer. That is only one of the many reasons why we strongly recommend against professional psychotherapy. If Crabb truly changes beyond making adjustments in vocabulary and expression, we will be glad to declare him a changed man on the issue of professional counseling, the cure of souls, and the role of the church.

Crabb concludes his book *Connecting* by saying, "When problems that reflect physical or practical matters of living arise, a healthy community will gladly refer people to professional experts for help."[43] With this sentence from the final paragraph of his book, Crabb once more confuses physical (medical, organic, biological) issues with practical matters of living. This is a wide open door to professional psychological counseling for anything and everything, and it reflects the position Crabb has held from the beginning, developed in his books, and promoted throughout the church. The overwhelming, worldwide popularity of Crabb's work is a testimony to how far many in the church have drifted from the biblical care of souls and how much believers are willing to accept the very wisdom of men warned about in Scripture. (1 Cor. 2:4-8.)

Crabb's shifts and expansions have primarily to do with getting his psychological ideas into the church and integrating psychology and Christianity in such a way that church leaders can do even more than professionally-trained counselors. Crabb describes his present work this way:

All I am wanting to do is to respond to what I think is the very sad observation that there are likely more powerful people, people who meaningfully engage folks who are hurting in the counseling community than in the church leadership community.[44]

Crabb has a dream for helping elders to "meaningfully engage folks who are hurting" (i.e. do the inside work). He has developed his psychological ideology but is still working on implementing his dream of making the church function accordingly.

In his 1995 *Christianity Today* interview, Crabb says:

> At one level, I haven't got a clue to what I'm doing. But I have a couple of central convictions, and I don't think I've ever felt more directly led by the Lord. It leaves me feeling more scared than I've ever felt in my life, but also more excited.[45]

People should not be fooled by that statement into thinking Crabb no longer has a psychologically tainted understanding of people and process of change. Crabb may at the time of the interview been uncertain about how he might accomplish his plan throughout the church and what to emphasize to get the job done. Moreover, a certain confusion, masquerading as complexity, cannot be avoided when one is trying to mix man-made theories and therapies with God-breathed Scripture.

In the meantime, at least until his dream is realized, Crabb has assured his colleagues that he will continue to recommend professionally trained counselors.[46] Psychological counselors have nothing to fear. Crabb continues to say that "there is still a good and honorable place for professional counseling in our society" and that "trained counselors have a legitimate role to play in healing the souls of struggling Christians."[47]

Even if Crabb's dream of training elders and shepherds to process fellow Christians in a church community comes true, Crabb would no doubt continue to recommend professional counselors as long as they are "powerful people," those who can see inside another person, expose the sinful strategies, and release the good capacities.

3

Self-Disclosure,
Exposure and
Community

The popular technique of self-disclosure can be seen in numerous books written by psychological therapists and others who believe in the importance of exposing the inner life. This self-disclosure invites the reader to enter the inner experiences of the writer for several purposes. Self-disclosure gives the impression that the therapist has experienced inner fears, thoughts and pain similar to that of the reader. It gives the impression that the writer is both approachable and knowledgeable about the inner life. And, it serves as an encouragement to the reader that exposing these fears, thoughts, and pain will bring greater self-understanding and thus psychological healing and health.

While it may appear that the writer is baring all and letting the reader see who he really is on the inside, the writer chooses what to expose and disclose for the purpose of the book. While he may appear to be letting his psyche show, he is actually revealing those thoughts and feelings he wants to talk about and wants the reader to think about. Moreover, it is a means of connecting with the reader in the same way that psychological counselors who have been influenced by theorists such as Carl Rogers attempt to connect with the counseling client. Rogers says:

> I hypothesize that personal growth is facilitated when the counselor is what he is, when in the relationship with his client he is genuine and without "front" or facade, openly being the feelings and attitudes which at that moment are flowing in him. We have used the term "congruence" to try to describe this condition. By this we mean that the feelings the counselor is experiencing are available to him, available to his awareness, that he is able to live these feelings, be them in relationship, and able to communicate them if appropriate. It means that he comes into a direct personal encounter with his client meeting him on a person-to-person basis. It means that he is being himself, not denying himself.[1]

This popular trend in writing gives the impression that the author is indeed in touch with his own inner life. He has progressed in bringing important aspects of his so-called unconscious into conscious awareness. He can now help others become both aware and accepting of the darkness and pain lurking beneath the surface. Writing in this mode is an attempt to reveal one's inner life for the purpose of encouraging the reader to be willing to face what psychiatrist Carl Jung referred to as the "dark side." Thus we read about haunting fears, feelings and thoughts expressed in the most wrenching, but eloquent terms—much like the sophomoric poetry we wrote as teenagers, focusing on inner pain and agony, even if there was only a modicum from which to draw. Somehow that seemed to be the only emotion worthy of poetry during those adolescent years. But now it is in vogue among adults who should have outgrown such maudlin self-focusing.

Crabb follows this technique in several of his more recent books. In his book *Finding God*, Crabb says, "In spite of passionate pleas for maturity, I'm still a mess." Crabb continues in this vein for several paragraphs including the following:

> For years, I have lived through seasons of self-hatred when I feel unwanted and unwantable. This self-loathing feels like a poisoned apple: Observe me from a distance and you may think me desirable. Get close enough to handle me and still I look good. Bite into me and you'll be harmed, perhaps destroyed. These poisonous feelings severely distort my thinking, drain me of productive energy, and shut me up in the perverse joys of sulking.[2]

But lest his readers get only a glimpse of his painful inside feelings, he assures them of his success as a person. He says:

> People who know me would say that I am painting an unfairly harsh picture of myself. And, happily, I agree. All that I've said is true, but I'm not telling the whole story. I gratefully acknowledge that I am

> a generous person, often thoughtful, sometimes sac-
> rificially kind. I work hard. I am deeply committed
> to my family. I am serious about my faith. I am nei-
> ther dishonest on my tax forms nor immoral in
> motel rooms. I have made an impact on others' lives.
> I know more of God now than I ever have before.[3]

Notice the appeal. It is to Christians who might not
think of themselves as problem-laden, as well as all those
who agonize internally. Crabb presents a partial picture
of his inner feelings and a partial picture of his outer life.
He draws the reader into finding God by exploring inner
feelings, but he retains his reputation, which is necessary
for the reader to have confidence in his proposed plan for
finding God.

Crabb's use of exposure has never been for the purpose of leaving people there or even for the purpose of
only understanding themselves. His purpose throughout
his books has been to use such exposure and psychological self-understanding for the purpose of change and
growth in knowing and depending on God. The idea of
God meeting the powerful motivating needs in the unconscious continues to be a theme. In *Finding God* he says:

> It has been nearly two years since I prayed, "Lord, I
> know you're all I have, but I don't know you well
> enough for you to be all I need. Please let me find
> you." In that time it has become more clear to me
> that neither spiritual discipline nor self-exploration
> carries me where I want to go. Confessing sins, rec-
> onciling with estranged friends, and spending regu-
> lar time in the Word are all necessary and right, But
> the more I wrestle with life as it really is, the more I
> am aware that living a spiritually disciplined life

develops at best only a nodding acquaintance with God.[4]

Notice how the usual Christian disciplines set forth in Scripture are not in themselves enough for Crabb. He contends that something more is needed. It is still looking inside, but he has added another dimension in *Finding God*, and that is looking inside for the good as well as the bad,[5] a theme he further develops in his later books.

Readers may be confused about Crabb's continued commitment to exploring and exposing the self when he says:

> Exploring my motives more thoroughly or rummaging through my past to dredge up connections between childhood hurts and present struggles provokes more frustration than hope. This self-examination may help me to know *myself* better, but I want to know God.[6] (Italics his.)

But, he is still not opposed to this activity, because "This self-examination may help me to know *myself* better." It is not that he has discarded such self-examination. It is that he wants to go further. Thus he presents the way, which he calls "a third option—an approach that equips us to dive into the cesspool of the human heart, find hidden treasure, and come up laughing," an approach that still "requires that we face the fallen structure in all of its loathsome , stubborn, wicked power and submit to a painful process of dismantling."[7]

Crabb is still in the business of exposing the contents of the unconscious for the purpose of dismantling the hidden beliefs and motives that prevent one from fully trusting God. He proposes a psychologically contaminated means, which serves as a deceptive counterfeit to

Ephesians 4:22-24 for putting off "concerning the former
conversation the old man, which is corrupt according to
the deceitful lusts," being "renewed in the spirit of your
mind," and putting on "the new man, which after God is
created in righteousness and true holiness."

Crabb reveals more about his own personal struggle
in *Hope When You're Hurting*, which he coauthored with
Dan Allender. He titles his first chapter "Why am I Still
Struggling So Much?" He writes his early chapters in the
first person singular and plural to help establish a connection of mutual struggle. After sharing his own struggles with fatigue, weariness and discouragement, he
explores various places hurting people look for help. He
leads his readers from one limited possibility of help to
another. Crabb does not paint a very hopeful picture as
he describes each category of limited help. The reader
must read on to the end of the book in search of hope if
he's hurting. But then, the reader ends up with the conclusion that until Crabb's "dream of what community
could provide for its members" is realized, the only hope
these days for people who can't find help by themselves,
through their natural community, or God, is professional
counseling.

Crabb's self-disclosure continues in his book *Connecting*, in which he includes the following quotation from
Henri Nouwen, a priest who was trained "as a psychologist and a theologian."[8] Nouwen says:

> That was a time of extreme anguish, during
> which I wondered whether I would be able to hold
> on to my own life. Everything came crashing down—
> my self-esteem, my energy to love and work, my
> sense of being loved, my hope for healing, my trust
> in God . . . everything. Here I was a writer about the
> spiritual life, known as someone who loves God and

gives hope to people, flat on the ground and in total darkness.

I experienced myself as a useless, unloved, and despicable person. Just when people were putting their arms around me, I saw the endless depth of my human misery and felt that there was nothing worth living for. All had become darkness. Within me there was one long scream coming from a place I didn't know existed, a place full of demons.[9]

Following the quote, Crabb says:

Not many could describe it as eloquently as Nouwen, but most of us know what it is to look in the mirror and see someone despicable, to listen to the deep places we try to pretend aren't there and hear one long scream of despair.[10]

Nevertheless Crabb does wax eloquent. He relates how during lunch with a friend, "I chose to share that I was living in a tunnel of discouragement so dark that I had no energy left to keep moving," and then remarks that people tend to be uncomfortable when faced with the inner life of another person.

We do not deny that people do experience agony in the depths of their being or the dark night of the soul. However, we believe that writing about it from a psychological perspective and explaining it from a mixed psychological-spiritual perspective is not useful or edifying to the body of Christ. Nor do we believe this is the biblical way of mutual ministry in the body of Christ.

Community or Encounter?

Crabb contends that Christians must talk about their inner life with one another if there is to be genuine help and authentic growth. Moreover, he sees that much good can be accomplished in the church if certain resources were to be released. He declares:

> I have been captured by the idea that God has placed extraordinary resources within us that have the power to heal us and our relationships. If released they could do a lot of good that we now think only trained specialists can accomplish.[11]

The resources to which Crabb is referring are the so-called God-given abilities for connecting with one another in community in such a way that people will be able to tell their stories in an environment of acceptance so that their badness may be faced and their goodness brought to the surface. While it is true that God has indeed "placed extraordinary resources within us that have the power to heal us and our relationships," Crabb's resources include psychodynamic overtones of talking about ourselves, exposing what lies hidden beneath the surface, repenting from unconscious strategies to protect ourselves from pain, and the release of gems of goodness that have been buried with all the pain of unmet needs.

There are some distinct similarities between Crabb's goal for community and the encounter movement. One of the basic assumptions of most encounter groups through the years has been that it is emotionally beneficial to be totally transparent and open. Self-exposure became a therapeutic absolute during the encounter movement and continues today in groups that attempt to connect people with one another in such a way that people will change and grow. Psychiatrist M. Scott Peck fondly recalls his encounter group experience. He says:

> We were a very diverse group of people, we sixteen. The first three days were spent in intense struggle. It was not boring. But it was often anxious, often unpleasant, and there was much anger expressed, at times almost viciously. But on the fourth day something happened, and I remember the suddenness of the shift. Suddenly we all cared for each other. Thereafter some cried and a couple wept. . . . I felt very safe in the T-group.[12]

Peck recalls that on the tenth day he felt depressed and the psychiatrist leader reminded him of their mutual beliefs as psychiatrists that depression could mask anger. The leader began pressing him into facing and expressing his anger. He broke down and wept openly, for the first time in many years, in this contrived community of the encounter group. In looking back on the event he says:

> Once again I had stumbled into community; and quite apart from the joy I felt, the freedom to be myself, the experience had changed the course of my life. For the first time I became aware of the healing power of genuine community. Many are aware of this power.[13]

Peck says:

> My T-group experience was a part of the "sensitivity group movement" that swept this country in the sixties and early seventies. That movement has largely died. One of the reasons for its death is that a great

many people found their sensitivity group experiences profoundly unpleasant. In the name of "sensitivity," confrontation was more encouraged than love.[14]

Nevertheless for Peck his encounter group experience was an inspiration for his book on people connecting in communities for healing. A number of therapists have been searching for a kind of community that was briefly experienced in encounter groups where people could be open, because they, along with Crabb, believe that we need to tell our stories, be open about our feelings and fears, and face our hidden inner forces in the company of people who will accept us no matter what we say.

While Crabb would be critical of various aspects of the encounter movement, he appears to be creating an environment for openness similar to the encounter groups. Only he wants to develop an environment of acceptance for the openness to bring forth the gems of goodness buried beneath hidden pain and strategies. As with those who saw some of the errors of the encounter movement, Crabb nevertheless seems to be looking for a similar kind of environment for change that Peck found in his encounter group experience.

Connecting in community is Crabb's expanded way to help people. He contends that "the absolute center of all powerful attempts to impact people for good is connecting."[15] We thought the absolute center was Christ, but for Crabb it is his psychospiritual process of connecting through community.

Telling our stories is Crabb's means of connection, not just for the purpose of getting to know one another better, but for the purpose of revealing inner pain, doubt, and strategies to deny the pain and then releasing what he refers to as our "lost glory." As people tell their stories according to Crabb's system, they try to help one another probe deeply into the inner person to expose the bad and release the good.

When people share their hurt and pain, they often end up sharing the sins of others. Crabb begins the first chapter of *Connecting* by exposing the failures of his son Kep. Usually when people are encouraged to talk about themselves, they talk about how others have hurt, failed or disappointed them. But in this instance Crabb uses it to model the way a powerful person can connect with another by accepting him in the midst of sin.[16]

Crabb believes that powerful people can help God transform the saints by probing around on the inside. He says:

> I recommend that we probe to discover what God is up to and join him in nourishing the life he has already given. It may be necessary to face what's wrong, not to make the wrong better, but to cut through it to find what's right.[17]

Thus probing is still part of the process.

> When you see me filled with doubt and self-hatred, when you observe me during my worst seasons of discouragement and failure, I want to be filled with both anguish (weep with me as I weep) and hope, not the empty hope that says trite things like "It'll all work out" or "Just hang in there—I'm sure you'll feel better soon," but a hope that exists because it sees something in me that is absolutely terrific.[18]

Once again, the humanistic focus is on what is "absolutely terrific" in "me."

Crabb's earlier teaching about people being image bearers, who somehow retain something of worth not sinful in itself, is repeated here as "lost glory in ourselves":

> What would it be like if we had a vision for each other, if we could see the **lost glory** in ourselves, our family, and our friends? What would the effect on your sons or daughters be if they realized that you were caught up with the possibilities of restored glory, of what they could become—not successful, talented, good-looking, or rich but kind, strong, and self-assured, fully alive.[19] (Bold added.)

The idea of worth (expressed in two needs) in Crabb's earlier books is here transformed into "lost glory" from Adam and Eve having been created in the image of God. But, when Christians are born again they do not regain a "lost glory" in themselves that they once had and later lost. Furthermore, this concentration on the goodness of the person instead of the goodness of Christ comes from the influence of psychology on Crabb's teachings.

Crabb declares:

> The deepest urge in every human heart is to be in relationship with someone who absolutely delights in us, someone with resources we lack who has no greater joy than giving to us, someone who respects us enough to require us to use everything we receive for the good of others, and because he has given it to us, knows we have something to give. The **longing to connect defines our digni**ty as human beings and our destiny as image-bearers.[20] (Bold added.)

He says, "Everyone shares the same longing."[21] Crabb's early teachings about the universal need for worth is now recast as the "longing to connect" that "defines our dignity." In other books this is stated as longings for relationship and impact. Thus, Crabb continues a similar theme related to needs resident in the image of God.

In this expanded probing, the sins of others are exposed along with the person's own pain and sinful strategies to deny the pain so that the goodness of the person is revealed. Thus even as Crabb teaches that there are " two sets of urges within us, good passions and bad passions"[22] and that "these urges seem to have a life of their own,"[23] exposing other people's sins helps a person discover his own goodness.

According to Crabb's dream, the church must become a community, somewhat like that described by Peck in his book *The Different Drum*. Only then, as people tell their stories will they be able to connect with God and with each other. Crabb says:

> Beneath all our problems, there are desperately hurting souls that must find the nourishment only community can provide—or die.[24]

Crabb rightly sees that individual counseling falls short of what the church can do, because there is a much deeper problem that psychological counseling cannot touch. He says:

> We must do something other than train professional experts to fix damaged psyches. Damaged psyches aren't the problem. The problem beneath our struggles is a disconnected soul. And we must do something more than exhort people to do what's right and then hold them accountable.[25]

Crabb is partly correct in saying, "The problem beneath our struggles is a disconnected soul." Indeed, those who are disconnected from God are "dead in their trespasses and sins." Only God can save them from the horror of separation from God and he does that through what Paul refers to as "the foolishness of preaching." It is God who saves and sanctifies, but not through a community that has learned the twentieth-century techniques of encounter groups or other psychological experiments in community.

And, we agree that "we must do something more than exhort people to do what's right and then hold them accountable." The Bible has been clear all along, without the help of Rogers' positive regard teachings, that the essence of being a Christian can be summed up in the word *love*. Jesus said, "This is my commandment, That ye love one another, as I have loved you" (John 15:12).

This love among the saints is generally absent in professional counseling. For years we have contended that people unnecessarily pay so-called experts to do what believers are called and already equipped to do, if they are growing in their walk with the Lord and walking according to the Spirit as presented throughout the Gospels and Epistles. However, Crabb writes this book as though believers do not know how to love one another for the complete work of God to be accomplished, as if they need help from the psychological community in order to learn how to connect.

It may be that many Christians have not grown in their love for God or in their love for one another, and it may be that many who profess to be Christians have not truly been born again. But, what Crabb presents in *Connecting* is contaminated with his commitment to psychological teachings about the nature of man and how he changes. While Crabb does not say that the sources for these ideas are from the psychological community, one can see the specter of psychology behind much of what he says. For instance, Crabb says:

> It's about time to free ourselves from the pressure that moralism creates and to tone down our preoccupying fascination with our internal workings, whether with psychological dynamics or with the subtleties of idolatry, a fascination that therapy often encourages.[26]

What does Crabb mean by "the pressure that moralism creates"? Does that mean we are to dismiss the moralism found in Proverbs and other sections of Scripture so that we won't feel guilty and pressured to repent? Humanistic psychologists have turned such words as *moralism*, *should*, and *ought* into bad words. Thus, Crabb says, "It's about time to free ourselves from the pressure that moralism creates." However, he only says to "tone down our preoccupying fascination with our internal workings, whether with psychological dynamics or with the subtleties of idolatry, a fascination that therapy often encourages." He says only to tone it down because it is still necessary according to Crabb's scheme. However, here he indicates that he has even more to offer than professional counseling, which he strongly supports.

Crabb still encourages people to look inside, to tell one another about what's hidden beneath the surface and to talk about the sins committed by others against them. He says:

> I want us to be honest about the insecurities, fears, and inadequacies that lie hidden in our hearts, beneath the appearances we may present to others.

I want us to speak with neither shame nor pride about the dark nights of our soul. I want us to be able to tell the stories of our abuse, rejection, or failure to a few special people who will listen and know they can't take the pain away, to people who will not think something is wrong with us that a therapist can fix and who will not simply tell us to get a grip on things.[27]

Crabb is still encouraging people to look beneath the surface, to expose and disclose the deepest parts of one's inner being. But now, in addition to doing this in the counseling office, Crabb has a dream for this to be done in the church where people can tell about their "abuse, rejection, or failure to a few special people who will listen and know they can't take the pain away, to people who will not think something is wrong with us that a therapist can fix and who will not simply tell us to get a grip on things."

Training Powerful People for Community

Crabb declares, "Ordinary people have the power to change other people's lives." He has said this from the very beginning, but it has always been qualified regarding who can do what and what training might be necessary for the deep inner work. In this book he says that "only a few people seem to possess" the power to powerfully change the life of a person with deep needs.[28] He asks:

What does it take to be a powerful person, someone who connects so deeply with another that power comes out of my being that enables the other to rise up with a new sense of vitality—and maybe with a "cure" for whatever psychological disorder was thought to be present? Can we all become powerful enough to stir up life in one or two others?[29]

Crabb proposes a plan to equip those he refers to as powerful people in the body of Christ to do this very thing. His plans to train pastors, elders and other Christians are clear in the name of his organization: the Institute for Biblical Community, formerly called the Institute of Biblical Counseling. In addition, he is conducting seminars to teach Christians his methods, referred to as "a better way."

The ad for two of Crabb's 1998 seminars, presented by his Institute for Biblical Community, asks: "What should the church be doing to meet the discipling and counseling needs of its people?"[30] Then he lists:

° Refer to professional counselors?
° Strengthen support groups?
° Hire more pastors?
° Develop lay counselors?
° Structure more discipling programs?

In answer to those possibilities, the add says:

In addition to using these methods, MAYBE THERE IS A BETTER WAY that we've overlooked. God has placed within His people the Power to change lives that is released when we learn to relate in ways that only the gospel makes possible when we learn to CONNECT. (Emphasis his.)

Observe that the "BETTER WAY" does not cancel referring to professional counselors or cancel developing lay counselors according to Crabb's methods. Instead, Crabb's "better way" is like his other "better" ways. Once again it is combining what he knows of living the Christian life with what he knows from studying psychology. He has attempted to make psychological counseling better by adding the Bible. He has attempted to make Christianity better by adding psychology. This is a further attempt to improve on Christianity by adding the psychological means of connecting in community.

Crabb's approach is different from the way Christianity was lived throughout the centuries. Aspects of his approach are concurrent with the current psychological trend of building community and of emphasizing what is good in the person, as well as exposing the pain of the past and the so-called ego-defense mechanisms. The ad refers to Crabb's "RADICAL NEW APPROACH to helping all of us deal with our personal struggles, an approach that depends for its power on SUPERNATURALLY CONNECTING in relationships that are possible for every believer." While he says that this "RADICAL NEW APPROACH" depends on "SUPERNATURALLY CONNECTING," his "RADICAL NEW APPROACH" also depends on psychological theories.

Notice also that this is for all believers. Crabb's "RADICAL NEW APPROACH" is for every believer, not just those who are experiencing difficult problems. He wants all believers to delve into the depths of the psyche to find the unmet needs, pain, disappointments, and strategies to avoid the pain (ego-defense mechanisms). He also wants them to find that "there is something good beneath the mess."[31] Here we have an extension of Crabb's psychological means for sanctification. He presented a "better way" of sanctification in *Understanding People* and *Inside Out*. He presented a "better way," which he referred to as "a third way" for finding God. And now he presents his "better way" for all believers to relate powerfully with God, self and others.

For Crabb the gospel of Christ "connects us to God, to ourselves, and to others."[32] But, where in Scripture does the gospel connect a person to himself? That is an addition from psychological theories about the nature of man and how he changes. The gospel gives new life and declares the old man dead, but there is no indication in Scripture that a human being is to connect to himself. While some of Crabb's goals for believers may appear admirable, his doctrines and his vision for the church are psychotherapeutically bound. They are what we call psychoheresy.

Crabb admits that he has "put a great deal of stock in self-awareness"[33] and justifies it by saying that God's "Spirit does search our hearts for hidden matters that interfere with trust."[34] But if God's Holy Spirit does the searching, there is no need for Christians to do that to one another. Yet, Crabb has relied on psychological means to expose the so-called unconscious and bring its contents to awareness. He continues to do so through his "better way" as he shows people how to develop community. While God does indeed work through members of the body of Christ, His pure revelation of Himself and of each individual is through His Word and Spirit. When God uses His church to expose hidden sin, it is through His Spirit and Word, not through psychological means of confronting and exposing in an atmosphere of Rogerian unconditional positive regard. Moreover, the sin is not hidden from the person in some dark cavern that can only be opened by some psychological open sesame.

Gospel of Self-Revelation

Crabb calls for the church to become a community with powerful people who can deal with the hidden realm of the psyche. He believes that God reveals Himself through those believers who understand and reveal their own inner selves and who will help others to become aware of all that lies hidden beneath their problems, i.e. in the unconscious. He says;

> But the *absolute center of what he* [God] *does to help us change is to reveal himself to us, to give us a taste of what he's really like, and to pour his life into us.* And a critical element in the revealing process is to place us in a community of people who are enough like him to give us that taste firsthand. If that is true, if a powerful experience of God comes through others, then connecting plays a vital, indispensable, powerful role in effectively addressing the **core issues of our souls, the issues that lie beneath all our personal, emotional, and psychological problems.**[35] (Italics his; bold added.)

Crabb thus uses God in his plan of revealing the hidden cavern of the unconscious. Crabb not only involves God in what he is doing, but he has added to the Word of God so that people can see God in the same way Crabb sees him.

In establishing his idea of community, Crabb reduces the Eternal God who is One God in Three Persons to an "the Eternal Community."[36] The Bible speaks of "the eternal purpose which he purposed in Christ Jesus our Lord" (Eph. 3:11), but Crabb presents his own version of how the Godhead established these eternal purposes. He refers to the "the Eternal Community" calling "a meeting."[37] Then Crabb has the audacity to script the words he imagines were spoken by the Father, Son, and Holy Spirit. In addition to contriving a script for God speaking, Crabb adds the accompanying human emotions, "and here the Father's voice broke."[38] While it may seem that Crabb makes God approachable, his script also trivializes God's majesty and holiness by reducing the Trinity to a community of three operating by consensus.

A brief reading of Crabb's rendition of God establishing his plan reduces God to three very human-sounding people meeting together to develop a plan in which God will create creatures with needs that cannot be met in the state of disconnection. But the Father will send the Son to bring these creatures into community. Jesus says how painful it will be, so painful that Crabb has Jesus say, "I cannot imagine what the actual experience will be like of not seeing your face."[39] What does this say about eternity, foreknowledge, and knowing the end from the beginning? Crabb even has the eternal Son, while yet in his perfect deity and without yet becoming man, question God's plans by asking, "There is no other way?"[40] Crabb also has the Son and Spirit express how delighted and thrilled they are to follow the plan set forth in the meeting. Thus, as in communities that work together, there is consensus.

Crabb ends his imaginary script with the Eternal Father saying, "It's time to get started. Let's see what we can do with this bit of clay. I have a vision for what it could become."[41] Does this even match what God, who is outside time and knows the end from the beginning, might say in one's wildest imagination? But Crabb's script works well for making his plan for community look the same as God's eternal purpose.

Where did Crabb get this extrabiblical "revelation"? From his own imagination! At the least it trivializes God and anthropomorphizes Him in a manner that Scripture does not. Worse yet, such writing is a dangerous encroachment on God's very being, a worldly handling of the holiness of God. Crabb misrepresents God's holy essence and eternal purposes.

Whenever people attempt to integrate psychotherapy and its underlying psychologies with Scripture they are in serious danger of distorting the gospel. The Bible is clear in its presentation of the human condition and God's solution through the gospel. While man was made in the image of God, every aspect of the image was tainted with the depravity of sin. Thus, the appeal of human worth, as if it is based on humanity being originally created in the image of God, is a distortion that came from secular psychological theorists who believe that a person's problems are based on a deep need for worth. Thus adding the psychological wisdom of man affects the true understanding of the human condition and how God saves and sanctifies.

The assumption that secular psychological theories about the nature of man have something helpful to add to the Bible undermines the Bible as the sole authority regarding who man is and how he changes. The Bible is the authoritative document on the doctrine of man, his fallen nature, salvation, sanctification, faith, and obedience. Adding extrabiblical notions about the inner workings of man from the opinions of unredeemed minds actually takes away from Scripture.

The confusion that arises when people try to integrate psychology with Christianity is not only an unclear gospel; it is a distorted gospel, even another gospel. At one point the writer may state the gospel in very biblical terms, but at other points the addition of psychological ideas distorts that very gospel. Throughout Crabb's books he has added psychological theories to the understanding of man. These may come across as theological statements. For instance he has Adam and Eve, "in their unfallen state, to long for grace that cannot yet be revealed."[42] Scripture does not support such longing before the Fall. Crabb's theories are about longings (needs, functioning powerfully from the unconscious) that originally existed in man when he was created in the image of God. Throughout his books, Crabb has presented man with powerful needs/longings/passions that motivate behavior outside the person's awareness. This Freudian-Adlerian-Maslowian notion lurks behind Crabb's theological understanding of the human condition.

Even though Crabb says that man sins, psychology distorts or confuses the nature of the sinner. Rather than clearly stating that the depravity of sin has tainted every part of man's being, Crabb presents sin as man's attempt to meet his needs apart from God. The needs/longings/passions are not presented as sinful. Instead, man's strategies for filling the needs and denying the pain of unmet needs are the sins. Thus, to stop sinning one must uncover what lies hidden in the psyche.

There is also a lack of clarity regarding human goodness. While on the one hand Crabb agrees that "all our righteousnesses are as filthy rags," some goodness seems to remain that needs to be found again, such as our "lost glory," which after salvation becomes "restored glory."[43] Crabb says about all people, saved and unsaved:

> The center of a biblical theory of personality is the idea of two sets of urges within us, good passions and bad passions, bad passions that exist because of the fall, good ones that are reliably present under the new covenant.[44]

Crabb further asserts that "these urges seem to have a life of their own"[45] and says:

> The bad urges in non-Christians, it should be noted, sink no lower than the bad ones in Christians, but the good ones don't reach as high.[46]

In other words the "good urges" of unbelievers are still good, but not as good. Elsewhere Crabb says:

> Christians now have two sets of inclinations, bad urges coming out of our flesh and good urges arising from our new hearts, the spirit that God has put within us.[47]

These two statements do not fit together unless there are good urges coming up from the flesh. This is just one example of how psychology distorts one's theology about the nature of man.

Crabb has added psychological ideas from need psychology about the nature of man, what must be changed and how it is to be changed. Rather than presenting people as sinners who must be given brand new life and a brand new heart, Crabb presents people as having to be convinced of God's love and His ability to meet their needs/longings/passion. Then once they are convinced the Holy Spirit's job is to "incline their hearts toward loving me [God] so that obedience will become a joy and not mere duty."[48] While on the one hand he says that Christ died for man's sins, Crabb stresses the purpose of Christ's death to be for convincing people of God's great love for them more than the purpose of Christ's death being an absolute necessity for God's holy justice to be fulfilled at the same time as His great mercy. God is love, but he is also holy, righteous and just. Every aspect of his nature was satisfied by Christ's propitiatory death on the cross. One must be careful not to give the impression that Christ's death was for the purpose of making God acceptable to man rather than making man acceptable to God, such as when Crabb has God saying:

> "Son, at just the right time I'll send you to become one of them and to accept the guilt for their sin. Then (and here the Father's voice broke) I'll break our connection and let you experience the death of separation from me that all sin deserves. When they see the extremes to which we will go to bring them into our community, the yearning we'll build into their hearts to be loved like that will draw them back to loving us fully and trusting us with their very souls."[49]

Nothing is even mentioned in Crabb's speaking for God about how grievously man sinned against God and violated His holiness or about the requirements of God's justice. Instead, Crabb has Christ die for "all that sin deserves" to let people "see the extremes to which we [Father, Son, and Holy Spirit] will go to bring them into our community." Nothing is said about people being convicted of sin as in the presentation of the gospel in Acts 2:37, where the people were "pricked in their heart." Instead the emphasis is on people being convinced of God's love and accepting Him as their meeter of needs and releaser of capacities. Also, how is it that people who are dead in their trespasses and sins can be drawn "back" to loving God, when the Bible says nothing about people loving God to begin with but everything about the inborn rebellion of every sinner?

Crabb's gospel presents mankind with an innate hidden yearning for God, which God fulfills by convincing people of His great love for them and by causing them to seek to have their needs met through Him. He emphasizes mankind's yet to be realized hidden worth and goodness and diminishes the depravity of man's sinful condition. This further diminishes the great work of Christ on the Cross and the full spectrum of God's glorious nature. Crabb's numerous psychological explanations and additions to God's Word and His saving and sanctifying work in the believer add up to a man-centered gospel. Crabb has transmogrified the truth of God by psychologizing the faith.

4

Integrating Psychology and the Bible

Crabb's rationale for integrating psychology with the Bible is based on his observation of superficial, ineffective Christians, his confidence in psychology, and his contention that the Bible does not give direct answers to people with problems of living. Crabb touches the common sense of the church when he points out the fact that there are Christians who are struggling with difficult problems of living. And, he touches the nerve of the church when he admonishes Christians for being materialistic and superficial. Christians can agree with him on a number of points. Yes, some Christians have serious problems of living. Yes, materialism and superficiality have greatly weakened individual Christians and the church as well. And Christians do need to grow in love for one another in the Body of Christ. They need to learn to walk in full dependence upon the Lord who is conforming each one to the image of Jesus Christ.

The Problem of Superficial Living.

We agree that there are serious problems in the church. Ineffective, superficial living does not honor Christ. Superficiality is not a new problem. Jesus faced that problem and said:

> Well hath Esaias prophesied of you hypocrites, as it is written, This people honoureth me with their lips, but their heart is far from me. Howbeit in vain do they worship me, teaching for doctrines the commandments of men. (Mark 7:6-7.)

Jesus did not mince words when he criticized religious leaders for masking their sinful hearts with an outward show of obedience. He saw the relationship between superficiality and replacing God's Word with man's wisdom.

> Woe unto you, scribes and Pharisees, hypocrites! for ye are like unto whited sepulchres, which indeed appear beautiful outward, but are within full of dead men's bones, and of all uncleanness. Even so ye also outwardly appear righteous unto men, but within ye are full of hypocrisy and iniquity. (Matthew 23:27-28.)

Jesus cried, "Woe," to the scribes and Pharisees, not only because of the deceitfulness of hypocrisy, but because of the eternal consequences of a disobedient heart.

Early in His ministry Jesus stressed the importance of the inner life of attitudes and motives. They were His central concern in His Sermon on the Mount. Notice how His opening words refer to the inner person.

> Blessed are the poor in spirit: for theirs is the kingdom of heaven.
> Blessed are they that mourn: for they shall be comforted.
> Blessed are the meek: for they shall inherit the earth.
> Blessed are they which do hunger and thirst after righteousness: for they shall be filled.
> Blessed are the merciful: for they shall obtain mercy.
> Blessed are the pure in heart: for they shall see God.
> Blessed are the peacemakers: for they shall be called the children of God. (Matthew 5:3-9.)

Such inner attitudes are not only receptive to the will of God, but bring forth fruitful actions. Therefore, we agree with Crabb when he declares that Christianity is more than outward actions.

We also agree with Crabb that superficiality is a serious problem. We say a hearty "Amen" to his plea for genuine love for one another in the Body of Christ. We also believe that Christians should be in the process of learning to walk in full dependence upon the Lord who saved us and who is conforming each one of us into the image of Jesus Christ. But, the inner man is not transformed into the likeness of Christ through psychological systems or techniques devised by men. The spiritual transformation of the inner man is outside of the domain of secularly based systems.

We agree with Crabb on the crucial importance of Christian sanctification being an inner work with outward consequences. However, we disagree with his psychological explanations and methods by which he hopes to achieve that inner change. While Crabb contends that his understanding about the nature and behavior of man is thoroughly biblical, his books reveal a heavy reliance on his background in clinical psychology. Though he claims to be a biblical counselor, his explanations and ways of change have been borrowed from psychology. On the one hand, he says that "the Scriptures provide the only authoritative information on counseling."[1] But, on the other hand he declares that "psychology and its specialized discipline of psychotherapy offer some valid insights about human behavior which," according to his own opinion, "in no way contradict Scripture."[2]

Like other integrationists, Crabb seeks to combine psychological theories and therapies with the Bible.[3] In his book *Effective Biblical Counseling*, he describes his method of integration as "Spoiling the Egyptians."[4] The label "Egyptians" represents psychological and psychiatric theorists. He argues that if a counselor will "carefully screen" concepts from psychology he will be able to determine their "compatibility with Christian presuppositions."[5] He contends that his method of screening will enable the church to glean "useful insights" from psychology without compromising commitment to Scripture. Crabb identifies his position as striking the balance between what he calls "Tossed Salad" (integrationists who are careless in their integration) and "Nothing Buttery" (those who have a "simplistic model of counseling" since it is based exclusively on the Word of God).[6] He claims that a Christian who spoils according to his guidelines "will be better equipped to counsel," than either the "Tossed Salad" or "Nothing Buttery" counselors.[7]

Problems with Integration

While an integrationist may truly admire the Bible, his reliance on psychology shows an equal, if not greater, confidence in secular theories and therapies and compromised confidence in the Scriptures as being in and of themselves sufficient for life and godliness. Integration implies that God gave commands without providing all the necessary means of obedience until the advent of psychology and indirectly faults God for leaving Israel and the church ill equipped for thousands of years until psychoanalytic and humanistic psychologists supplied the necessary insight. Mixing psychotherapy and its underlying psychologies with Scripture seems to discount the possibility of living the Christian life solely through spiritual means provided by God in His Word and through His Holy Spirit.

In contrast to the integrationist position, numerous passages extol the sufficiency, power, and excellency of God's Word. For instance 2 Peter 1:2-4 says:

> Grace and peace be multiplied unto you through the knowledge of God, and of Jesus our Lord, according as his divine power hath given unto us all things that pertain unto life and godliness, through the knowledge of him that hath called us to glory and virtue: Whereby are given unto us exceeding great and precious promises: that by these ye might be partakers of the divine nature, having escaped the corruption that is in the world through lust.

The Bible is not meant to work independently from God Himself. The Bible is sufficient because the Lord Himself works through His Word. If a person tries to use the Bible apart from Christ ruling in His heart, he may claim that the Bible lacks practical answers for life's difficulties. However, it is through the Bible that God reveals Himself and works His divine power in Christians' lives. The Bible is more than words on a page. Every word is backed by His mighty power, His perfect righteousness, His love, His grace, and His wisdom. Thus God not only gives precious promises and instructions for living; He enables a believer to obey His Word. That is why the Bible is sufficient for life and conduct.

Paul refused to depend on the wisdom of men, but on the power and wisdom of God. Not only is human wisdom foolishness in comparison with God's wisdom; human words lack the divine power necessary to transform a person into the likeness of Christ and to enable him to live the Christian life according to God's will. God uses the wisdom and power of the Scriptures to enable believers to please Him and bear fruit:

> All scripture is given by inspiration of God, and is profitable for doctrine, for reproof, for correction, for instruction in righteousness, that the man of God may be perfect, thoroughly furnished unto all good works. (2 Timothy 3:16-17.)

No psychological doctrine can even come close to that claim, nor can it add power for change. While sincere integrationists believe that there are psychological theories about the nature of man and therapies for change that do not contradict Scripture, the root remains the same. Jesus was always concerned about ungodly roots and about following the traditions of men instead of the Word of God. Paul also warned:

Beware lest any man spoil you through philosophy and vain deceit, after the tradition of men, after the rudiments of the world, and not after Christ. (Colossians 2:8.)

Thus the problem of the psychospiritual integrationist is the source from which he has borrowed: psychological counseling systems which were devised by agnostics and atheists to answer questions about the human condition without regard for the Creator and His Word.

A Sufficient Bible Without Direct Answers?

Crabb attempts to alleviate the problem of integration in the opening chapters of *Understanding People* by arguing that the sufficiency of Scripture means that it is sufficient as a framework. Then he proceeds to supplement that framework with psychological insights.[8] He says:

Yes, the Bible is sufficient to answer every question about life, but not because it **directly** responds to every **legitimate** question.[9] (Emphasis added.)

Then he argues that psychology can be used to fill in the direct information to unanswered questions that he regards as legitimate. Repeatedly using the terms *directly* and *legitimate*, he attempts to build a case for seeking definitive answers outside the Scriptures.

Crabb agrees that the Bible answers some important questions, but contends that it lacks the so-called direct information necessary to address the legitimate questions that real people ask about the harsh reality of their real world.[10] He says that "no passage literally exegeted directly responds" to a host of legitimate questions.[11]

Therefore one must supplement Scripture with creative thoughts gleaned from psychology to answer such questions.[12]

By such reasoning, Crabb seems to be saying that the Scriptures are both sufficient and insufficient. While claiming to believe in the sufficiency of Scripture, he goes outside of the Scriptures and turns to psychological opinions for answers to questions such as these:

> What am I supposed to do with my deep desire to be a woman because I'm so scared of being a man?
> How do I handle my terrible fear that if I ever expressed how I really feel, no one would really want me?
> Why do I feel so threatened when someone successfully proves that I've been wrong about something?
> Why do I not want to admit my internal struggles?[13]

In Crabb's opinion, the Bible does not clearly deal with questions being asked by desperate people.[14] He reasons that if one sticks only with the exegesis of Scripture he will not answer vital questions or else he will give only shallow and simplistic answers.[15]

According to Crabb, any counselor who does not address those questions has a "shallow understanding of problems and solutions that sounds biblical but helps very few."[16] In fact, he declares that a counselee could be "significantly harmed" if counseled by shallow thinkers who have not yet addressed those legitimate questions.[17] Crabb implies that counselees are entitled to answers to those legitimate questions, because if no one addresses their legitimate questions they will be forced to accept "superficial solutions."[18]

In *Understanding People* Crabb gives three illustrations which produce questions which he says that the literal exegesis of Scripture will not answer.[19] The three cases concern a man with desires to dress as a woman; a woman with sexual hang-ups; and an anorexic. The unanswered question is the same in each case, namely, why do they display such bizarre behavior? In Crabb's opinion the Bible does not directly answer this crucial, legitimate "why?"

With each of his three illustrations Crabb cites Scriptures prescribing the correct course of action which will please God.[20] The Scriptures directly tell each person **what** God desires them to do. But according to Crabb the Scriptures do not tell them what he considers to be the more crucial and fundamental matter: **Why** do people desire bizarre and sinful action? But contrary to Crabb, the Bible does not provide simplistic psychological answers. It answers the big "why?" Sinful behavior is the result of man's sinful nature.

It may be interesting to look at the great variety of psychological opinions when dealing with what Crabb identifies as "legitimate questions." But, the danger in looking for answers to such questions outside of the Bible is that psychological systems tend to place answers outside of the person himself. Because of the underlying philosophy that people are innately good and are corrupted by society, mainly parents, psychological theories look for reasons for unacceptable attitudes and behavior in circumstances outside of the person. **That is why those kinds of answers are not found in the Bible.** Even when Satan or other persons may tempt people to sin, God says through his word that even then they are drawn into sin by their own lust (James 1:14). God holds people responsible for their own sin. Thus, according to the Bible itself, it is neither necessary nor profitable to go outside

Scripture for answers. The Bible answers the truly crucial questions about the nature of man and why he
behaves the way he does.

Crabb complains about counselors who do not know or
use answers found in psychology. Such counselors have
before them God's clear word on the nature of man and
right conduct, but they do not have what Crabb would
consider a **direct** answer to the crucial question "Why?"
They use God's clear Word. They believe in pursuing obedience to God's will when He has spoken clearly on the
pleasing course of conduct. But, what does Crabb say of
such counsel? He condemns it as promoting mere "external conformity."[21] In fact, he contends that such counsel
would leave such people "utterly unhelped, and worse,
significantly harmed."[22] In his book *Connecting*, he says,
"It's about time to go beneath the moralism that assumes
the church's job is done when it instructs people in biblical principles and then exhorts them to do right."[23]

Evidently Crabb equates simple obedience to the
Word of God with superficiality, external conformity, and
ineffective moralism. Surely he does not think that the
Bible is limited to only external concerns! Obedience to
the law of the Spirit in Christ Jesus (Romans 8:2)
includes both inner and outer obedience. In fact Paul's
explanation of walking according to the Spirit in Romans
8 deals with the inner life and motivation, not with anything superficial. How can one indict counsel from the
Bible alone as anything superficial or merely external?

One wonders about Crabb's severe criticism of Christians who have not yet dealt with his legitimate questions. What about those who have ministered through the
centuries without being privy to insights derived from
psychology which supposedly deal directly with Crabb's
legitimate questions? And what about Jesus?

Jesus would not have answered the questions according to any psychological theories even if they had been around. He does not excuse, justify, or fix up the old self. He enables His disciples to obey His commands by His own presence in their lives. He says:

> Abide in me, and I in you. As the branch cannot bear fruit of itself, except it abide in the vine; no more can ye, except ye abide in me. I am the vine, ye are the branches: he that abideth in me, and I in him, the same bringeth forth much fruit: for without me ye can do nothing. (John 15:4-5.)

But, Crabb proposes to transform the self through psychological insight, using the wisdom of the world for spiritual matters.

The Bible answers questions about human behavior in terms of God's holiness and man's depravity. Details of the old self-life may not be fully understood, but Jesus gives the way out of self and into Him. What Crabb identifies as legitimate questions may indeed be part of the load that Jesus wants His children to leave at the foot of the cross. The answer to all of the impediments and confusions of the old self-life is to come to Christ, to take His yoke of relationship and guidance, and to really know Him in a personal, vital way. Jesus says:

> Come unto me, all ye that labour and are heavy laden, and I will give you rest. Take my yoke upon you, and learn of me; for I am meek and lowly in heart: and ye shall find rest unto your souls. For my yoke is easy, and my burden is light. (Matthew 11:28-30.)

The Bible continually stresses that it is personal knowledge of the Father and the Son that leads to life and godliness, rather than details about the self that the Bible does not provide. And it is the Spirit who enables us to crucify self, that Christ may be glorified in and through us.

> There is therefore now no condemnation to them which are in Christ Jesus, who walk not after the flesh, but after the Spirit. For the law of the Spirit of life in Christ Jesus hath made me free from the law of sin and death. (Romans 8:1-2.)

The life of Jesus, mediated to us by the Holy Spirit, is the very source of the solution to each one of the above problems. Psychological answers are not only speculative, irrelevant and inconsequential; they are also misleading and can be ultimately destructive. The conflicting variety of answers from various psychologies illustrates how uncertain their answers really are. One psychological counselor's answer often disagrees sharply with another's, even if both of them are Christians. In contrast to the wide diversity of opinions among the various psychological systems, the Word of God is true, reliable, and life changing.

Such questions and their diverse psychological answers can actually become a smoke screen for not hearing and obeying God's will. They can easily prevent or delay a person from putting off the sinful self-life and putting on the righteousness of God through surrender to Him. Psychological explanations for behavior may actually serve to keep one from the radical change that God desires to bring through His Spirit. On the other hand, when a person comes to the point of desiring God's complete sovereignty in his life in every detail, the Lord will enable him to know and understand all that is essential for a life of holiness, godliness, and righteousness. God can do a far deeper work than any fanciful combination of psychological opinions about questions supposedly left out of Scripture.

Millions of Christians will never seek answers beyond the Bible to understand why they do what they do. Yet, they will obey God when the Spirit speaks through His Word. Surely the Spirit of God and the Word of God are not leading them to mere external conformity! Millions of Christians will never read Crabb's psychological answers as to the "why?" They will only be able to rely on their own relationship with God and the study of His Word. Surely the Spirit of God and the Word of God will not leave them with a shallow and deficient view of man! Millions of Christians will never enter into any more than study, memorization, and obedience to the direct statements of Scripture. Surely this does not mean that the Spirit of God and the Word of God can only lead them into a shallow, simplistic, and superficial method of ministering to one another.

A Biblical Approach to Problems of Living

A Christian's answer to problems of living depends on his relationship with God and obedience to His Word. If one starts with the premise of the absolute sufficiency of Scripture, then he will work out from the Bible into the world and its problems. It is a process of moving from Scripture into the world as led by the Holy Spirit. Thus, one who ministers biblically will view people and their problems through the lens of the Bible, not through the lenses of psychology. Those integrationists who use the double lenses of psychology and the Bible will only produce double vision. And how can counselors with double vision point out the right way to struggling Christians?

God does not interpret man according to such psychological ideology. Therefore the church should not use it. Certainly God was not ignorant of these matters when He guided His servants to record His Word. Surely God does not regret that Freud, Jung, Maslow, and others did not live in the first century so that his apostles might have incorporated their notions into the gospels and epistles. Nor is Paul's presentation of sanctification shallow and deficient because it lacks the so-called insights of psychological theory.

God never intended for His people to doubt the power and sufficiency of His Word. The Spirit says boldly that the Word of God can pierce to the core of man's being. Hebrews 4:12 declares:

> For the word of God is quick, and powerful, and sharper than any two-edged sword, piercing even to the dividing asunder of soul and spirit, and of the joints and marrow, and is a discerner of the thoughts and intents of the heart.

The Lord through His Word can transform an individual in a way that no psychologist could ever hope. Indeed the heart of man is deceitful and desperately wicked. It is beyond human ability to discern its wicked ways, as God says so forcefully in Jeremiah 17:9-10. However human depravity and treachery do not prevent the Word of God from doing what it says it will do. The Word and the Holy Spirit cut through to the inner man. God, who searches the heart and examines the mind, who discerns a person's thoughts from afar and knows our words before they are on our tongue, has spoken in the Bible.

The apostle Paul recognized that change on the inside is brought about through the Holy Spirit in conjunction with the Word of God. He prayed:

> That [the Father of our Lord Jesus Christ] would grant you, according to the riches of His glory, to be strengthened with might by His Spirit in the inner man; that Christ may dwell in your hearts by faith; that ye, being rooted and grounded in love, may be able to comprehend with all saints what is the breadth, and length, and depth, and height; and to know the love of Christ, which passeth knowledge, that ye might be filled with all the fulness of God. Now unto him that is able to do exceeding abundantly above all that we ask or think, according to the power that worketh in us, unto him be glory in the church by Christ Jesus throughout all ages, world without end. Amen. (Ephesians 3:16-20.)

Only Jesus' love and life bring about the kind of heart change that bears eternal fruit and that honors God instead of men. Jesus gave His own life to change people on the inside. He did not give a technique, but rather His very own life to will and do His own good pleasure in and through each believer. No psychotherapist or psychological technique can perform wonders akin to what Christ does through His Word and His Spirit!

5

The Use and Praise of Psychology

Crabb's confidence in psychology permeates his earlier books. But some of his followers believe that his later books indicate that he has moved away from his dependence upon psychological presuppositions, understandings, and techniques. Yet, his extensive indebtedness to psychology is as thorough in his most recent books as in earlier ones. In *Understanding People*, Crabb says, "Readers familiar with my earlier books will recognize movement in my concepts **but not, I think, fundamental change**."[1] (Emphasis added.) His subsequent books reveal a strong affiliation with psychological opinion and practice.

In *Effective Biblical Counseling*, after his defense of "Spoiling the Egyptians," Crabb recommends over twenty secular psychologists to help Christians become "better equipped to counsel."[2] Men such as Freud, Adler, Maslow, Rogers, et al. are extolled as potentially beneficial.[3] Crabb's belief that psychologists offer a substantive body of truth for the church can be seen in his own statements.[4]

> Again let me insist that psychology does offer real help to the Christian endeavoring to understand and solve personal problems.[5]

Crabb not only praises the movement as a whole but also exalts certain "bright lights" from within the camp. For example, Crabb sharply censures those who reject the psychological opinions of Carl Rogers,[6] even though it is difficult to follow Rogers' teachings without being influenced by the presuppositions which underlie them.

Crabb criticizes Rogers' humanistic goals, but does not hesitate to use those aspects of Rogers' theory and practice that appeal to him. This is the typical eclectic, integrationist position. In his 1997 book, *Connecting*, he says he is "drawn to the kind of community that Rogers envisions, where acceptance supplants judgment, where we continue calling out the good in each other in spite of whatever ugliness we see."[7] The interesting thing in this is that the kind of connection Rogers promoted was one that could be quickly established and easily left behind.

> The man of the future . . . will be living his transient life mostly in temporary relationships . . . he must be able to establish closeness quickly. He must be able to leave these close relationships behind without excessive conflict or mourning.[8]

Nevertheless, Crabb would like to see "Rogers's thinking rub off on pastors" and on himself.[9]

Special Praise for Freud and His Psychology

The Freudian concept of the unconscious serves as the cornerstone of Crabb's model of man and methodology of change. The Freudian *unconscious* is not simply an adjective to describe that part of the brain that stores bits of information which are not presently in awareness. In Freud's psychoanalytic theory, the unconscious is a reservoir of drives and impulses which govern an individual beyond his conscious awareness. Freud changed an adjective into a noun and thus gave it form and substance. The Freudian unconscious not only holds memories and information; it also motivates present thinking and acting. Furthermore, it is out of reach through ordinary mental activity.

Freud's use of the word *unconscious* is technical and specific. According to the *Dictionary of Psychology*, when *unconscious* is used as a noun it is "the region of the mind which is the seat of the id and of repressions." And when the word *unconscious* is used as an adjective in the technical sense, it is defined as "characterizing an activity for which the individual does not know the reason or motive for the act." It is a hidden, elusive part of man which supposedly "cannot be brought to awareness by ordinary means." It is supposedly the residence and source of a person's drives, motivations, actions, and even essence of life. "Thinking which goes on without awareness," "memories which have been forced out of the conscious level of mind into the unconscious," and "motivation of which the individual is unaware" are all part of Freud's creation of the unconscious.[10]

Crabb's use of the word *unconscious* is very similar to the above psychological description. His commitment to the Freudian theory of the unconscious is evident from the following quotations from *Understanding People*.

> Freud is rightly credited with introducing the whole idea of *psychodynamics* to the modern mind. The term refers to psychological forces within the personality (**usually unconscious**) that have the power to cause behavioral and emotional disturbance. He taught us to regard problems as *symptoms* of **underlying *dynamic processes* in the psyche**.[11] (Italics his; bold added.)

He continues, "I think Freud was correct. . . when he told us to look beneath surface problems to **hidden internal causes**." (Bold added.) Crabb does not agree with all that Freud taught and even sees errors in his theories, but he insists that "the error of Freud and other dynamic theorists is *not* an insistence that we pay close attention to **unconscious forces** within personality."[12] (Italics his; bold added.) In spite of Freud's rejection of Christianity, Crabb says, "I believe that [Freud's] psychodynamic theory is both provocative and valuable in recognizing elements in the human personality that many theologians have failed to see."[13]

In his earlier books Crabb uses the word *unconscious* directly and explains its hidden nature and power for motivation. In his book *Inside Out* he relies on metaphors and descriptive phrases such as "heart," "core," "beneath the surface," "hidden inner regions of our soul," "dark regions of our soul," "beneath the waterline," "underlying motivation," "hidden purpose," and "reservoir of their self-protective energy."[14] In fact the very title *Inside Out* points to the Freudian notion of the unconscious.[15] He affirms this in *Connecting*. He says:

> An earlier book of mine, *Inside Out*, offered a guided tour of our internal world. That tour revealed that we are always aching for something better and reliably sinning in our efforts to keep ourselves alive.[16]

Like Freud, Crabb clearly portrays the unconscious as a real and powerful part of every person. He further suggests that such doctrines of the unconscious are indispensable to the church.

Because of the influence of Freudian thought in our twentieth century culture, most people believe in some kind of unconscious. However, their interpretation of what the unconscious is or does will vary from one person to another. One person may do something out of habit and say he does it unconsciously. Or another may say that there must be an unconscious because he does not have to think about every single thing he does while driving a car.

On the other hand, Freud stated that the unconscious is a place where all kinds of powerful drives and mysterious motivations cause people to do what they do, whether they want to or not. The implications of such a powerful seat of urges driving people to do all kinds of things against their will flies in the face of God holding people responsible for their actions. If people look for unconscious reasons for their behavior, they can excuse all sorts of behavior. **But, the idea of the unconscious as a hidden region of the mind with powerful needs and motivational energy is not supported by the Bible or science.**

We are tremendously complex beings, but psychological explanations about the inner workings of the soul are

merely speculation. The only accurate source of information about the heart, soul, mind, will, and emotions is the
Bible. Not only is the Bible accurate; the Lord Himself
knows and understands exactly what lies hidden beneath
the surface of every person. He knows and He brings
cleansing to those inner parts that we may never understand. David prayed:

> Search me, O God, and know my heart: try me, and
> know my thoughts: and see if there be any wicked
> way in me, and lead me in the way everlasting.
> (Psalms 139:23-24.)

Teaching a Freudian concept of the unconscious is a
disservice to Christians. Rather than relying on the Word
of God and the indwelling Holy Spirit to search their
hearts, they will learn to rummage around in some kind
of Freudian unconscious and remain focused on the self.

Crabb does not merely praise the unverified notions of
Freud. He actually incorporates a Freudian type of
unconscious into the very heart of his teachings on sanctification. In a discussion entitled "The Beginnings of
Change" he presents the unconscious as the key element
of change.[17] He teaches that Christian growth comes
from **gaining insight into the unconscious**. Crabb
declares that failure to face the so-called reality of an
unconscious reservoir of "beliefs, images, and pain" will
result in "disastrous externalism."[18] He contends that
failure to deal fully with the "unconscious" will result in
"pressure, judgmentalism, legalism, and pride rather
than deep love for God and for others."[19]

Thus without Scriptural warrant, **Crabb teaches
that the unconscious is a crucial factor in sanctification.** Without providing a **biblical** definition of the
unconscious (aside from a misinterpretation of the bibli-

cal use of the word *heart*), Crabb makes it a central element of his counseling system. Even though he does not provide biblical verification for his view, Crabb criticizes pastors and other Christian leaders for failure to emphasize the unconscious.[20] According to Crabb, leaders who ignore this Freudian notion produce unconscious "robots or rebels" who ignorantly conform to external expectations while continuing in their unconscious rebellion.[21] Indeed, without the law of the Spirit of life in Christ Jesus (Romans 8:2) leaders can produce rebels and robots, whether or not they use psychological ideas of the unconscious.

Crabb suggests that ignorance of the crucial role of the unconscious allows error to spread throughout the entire evangelical church.[22] He says, "Perhaps the major error of evangelical churches today involves a shallow and deficient understanding of sin."[23] But his analysis of the problem is that the church has failed to grasp the absolute centrality of the unconscious. Crabb levels the blame for the spread of this "error" on church leaders who have ignored this Freudian notion. He explains:

> Many pastors preach an "iceberg view" of sin. All they worry about is what is visible above the water-line.[24]

There is a real problem when preachers concentrate on external things and ignore sinful motives, resentment, unforgiveness, self-will, self pity, and self-centeredness. However, Crabb is talking about ignoring the Freudian unconscious.

The iceberg is Freud's classic model of the unconscious. The entire iceberg represents the mind, and only the tip is accessible to the person. It includes all information and memories which are accessible through recall as well as present thoughts and mental activity. The huge mass beneath the waterline does not simply represent all that is presently outside conscious awareness. It supposedly contains all that drives, motivates, and determines behavior outside conscious volition. Psychologists Hilgard, Atkinson, and Atkinson point this out in their standard work on psychology.

> Freud compared the human mind to an iceberg: the small part that shows above the surface of the water represents conscious experience, while the much larger mass below water level represents the unconscious—a storehouse of impulses, passions, and inaccessible memories that affect our thoughts and behavior. It was this unconscious part of the mind that Freud sought to explore by the method of free association . . . . By analyzing free associations, including the recall of dreams and early childhood memories, Freud sought to help his patients become aware of much that had been unconscious and thereby to puzzle out the basic determinants of personality.[25]

This explanation of personhood is based on conjecture, not scientific investigation. Not only does this concept of the unconscious make it "a storehouse of impulses, passions, and inaccessible memories"; it also assigns power to "affect our thoughts and behavior." The bizarre interpretations that Freud placed on his patients' free associations, dreams, and memories illustrate the distortion that results from trying to rummage about in a so-called unconscious.[26]

Crabb confidently uses Freud's iceberg illustration to explain the mind and its contents.[27] Although he denies that his concept of the unconscious is "a derivative of secular Freudian thinking smuggled into Christian theology," his use of the iceberg image and metaphor reveals a Freudian view of the unconscious.[28] Crabb follows Freud when he teaches that the content above the water line represents the conscious mind, while the content below the water line represents the unconscious.[29] Crabb, like Freud, also assigns motivating power to the unconscious.

Crabb likens pastors who focus only on conscious activity to the ill-informed sea captain who steers his vessel around the tip of an iceberg while remaining ignorant of the existence of "a mountain of ice beneath the surface."[30] According to Crabb, those pastors fail to take into account the great mass of crucial material motivating the person from the unconscious. He also claims that evangelical Christianity's ignorance of that "great mass of sinful beliefs" and motives has produced a masquerading of spiritual health.[31]

The Influence of Anna Freud, Alfred Adler and Others

Freud's theory of the unconscious has had a profound influence on counseling psychology. His followers either elaborated or modified his doctrine of the unconscious. Freud's daughter Anna wrote extensively on ego-defense mechanisms of the unconscious, which include unconscious denial and repression. Crabb commends Anna Freud for her "classic work on ego-defense mechanisms," which play a significant role in his own system. He declares that her writings are "appropriate and helpful reading for a Christian."[32] The heavy emphasis on the defense mechanism of denial continues throughout all of Crabb's work. It is essential to *Understanding People* and for changing from the *Inside Out* and continues in his later books, *Finding God* and *Connecting*. In *Finding God*, Crabb declares:

> People who feel no deep passion have only buried it. They seal their desires beneath an impenetrable wrapping that keeps them from ever being touched. They may display a glib geniality, full of good humor and warm chatter, or they may present themselves as flat and colorless, entirely unengaged with anything that would provoke feelings.[33]

Yet, Freudian theory has met with growing criticism both in and out of the field of psychology. Furthermore, acceptance of Freud conflicts with the biblical view of conscious choice and responsibility. Therefore, Crabb is careful to say that he does not believe in unconscious *determinism* or its complement of early determinants of behavior. At first this seems like a contradiction. However, it is simply a modification of Freud's theory, similar to that found in Alfred Adler.

We are not accusing Crabb of being totally Freudian, because he does not incorporate the Oedipus Complex or the early psycho-sexual stages of development. However, one can see the Freudian influence in Crabb's theory that people are motivated by the contents of the unconscious. In the sense of the iceberg metaphor, the centrality of the unconscious is the same even though Crabb's content would be somewhat different from Freud's. **Just as with Freud's therapeutic system, eliminating the theory of the unconscious would be tantamount to eliminating Crabb's entire system as well.**

Crabb's adaptation of the Freudian unconscious is much the same as Alfred Adler's (a follower of Freud). Like Adler, Crabb teaches that while people are responsible and make choices, their unconscious motives direct a substantial amount of behavior. In like manner, Crabb also teaches that unconscious motives often result in self-defeating behaviors. Like Adler, Crabb promotes a combination of unconscious motivation and personal responsibility and insists that a person be held responsible for wrong attitudes and actions which originate from wrong assumptions in the unconscious.

The following is a brief overview of Adler's theory:

> Adler's theory shared some of psychoanalysis's [Freud's] tenets: psychic determinism, the purposeful nature of behavior, the existence of many motives outside conscious awareness, and the notions that dreams could be understood as a mental product, and that insight into one's own unconscious motives and assumptions had curative power. Adler, however, rejected the energy model of libido and replaced it with a future-oriented model of striving toward a subjectively determined position of significance. . . . Adler's human was an active striver trying to cope with the tasks of life but hampered by mistaken apperceptions and faulty values.[34]

Keep this in mind as we examine the details of Crabb's system. Adler's influence on Crabb's integration model of counseling is seen in his emphasis on the need to promote insight in order to move a counselee beyond hidden motives underlying behavior. Adler says, "Fundamental changes are produced only by means of an exceedingly high degree of introspection."[35] Adler further declares:

> . . . individual-psychology can intervene to some purpose, and by means of an intensified introspec-

tion and an extension of consciousness, secure the domination of the intellect over divergent and hitherto unconscious stirrings.[36]

Similarly Crabb contends that we need the help of another person to accomplish deep change through intensified introspection. Just as Adler used both individual and group therapy, so does Crabb. The emphasis on exposing contents of another's unconscious for the purpose of insight and therefore growth is very similar to Adler.[37] In *Finding God* Crabb says:

> We must learn to tell the story of our lives—the good, the bad, and the ugly—to explore who we are: twisted image-bearers who live together in a community of other twisted image-bearers in the presence of an untwisted God, who is slowly making us straight. We will never find God by denying who we are and where we've been.[38]

Adler's influence on Crabb concerning what neither would like to refer to as early determinants of behavior can be seen in Crabb's adaptation of Adler's "Early [childhood] Recollection Technique."[39] In this technique the counselor asks the counselee to recall and describe early painful memories in order to find a key to present feelings and behavior. This projective technique supposedly provides insight into the direction and meaning of life.[40] However, as with all projective techniques, it is simply creative guess work, a kind of creative feeling around in the dark caverns of the Freudian unconscious in search of light.

Crabb has also been influenced by Adler's theories concerning the direction of movement, self-defeating behaviors, unrealistic assumptions, denial, and safe-guarding tendencies. In *Finding God* Crabb says:

> We are passionately determined to make our lives
> less painful, and we will do whatever it takes to
> reach this goal in a disappointing, sometimes plea-
> surable, and maddeningly uncertain world.[41]

Adler emphasized that all behavior is directed to the goal of overcoming inferiority and thereby gaining a sense of worthwhileness in both relationship and tasks of life. Similarly Crabb teaches that all behavior is moti-vated by needs for worthwhileness through security (rela-tionship) and significance (impact).

Crabb also follows Adler in the emphasis on emotion. Adler believed that emotions are aroused when a person gains real insight into his own hidden motives, wrong assumptions, use of denial and other safe-guarding tech-niques.[42] Later when we consider Crabb's methods of change we will see the strong emphasis on feeling pain from the past. Crabb's stories about people resisting insight therapy into the hidden regions of the uncon-scious also follow Adler's explanations concerning counse-lees resisting treatment through self-protecting strategies.[43]

Freud greatly influenced Adler, especially in terms of the importance of unconscious motivations. Then Adler influenced a number of other psychological theorists, including Karen Horney, Carl Rogers, and Albert Ellis.[44] Basic assumptions of these psychologists as well as those of Abraham Maslow hold predominant places in Crabb's system.

Albert Ellis's Rational Emotive Therapy (now called Rational Emotive Behavior Therapy) appears to have played a significant role in the development of Crabb's

Rational Circle. He teaches that thoughts about oneself greatly affect behavior. And, since Ellis is an avowed humanist, his teachings are centered in self. He not only leaves God out of the picture, but says that "unbelief, humanism, skepticism, and even thoroughgoing atheism not only abet but are practically synonymous with mental health" and that "devout belief, dogmatism, and religiosity distinctly contribute to, and in some ways are equal to, mental or emotional disturbance."[45] For Ellis, self-interest is better than self-sacrifice, and unconditional self-acceptance is a prime feature of mental health. He says:

> Nonreligious philosophies, like RET, teach that you can always choose to accept yourself *because* you decide to do so, and that you require no conditions or redundant beliefs in God or religion to help you do this choosing.[46] (Italics his.)

Then Ellis puts down those Christians who try to combine Christianity with teachings on self-acceptance by saying:

> Ironically, when you do decide to adopt a religious view and choose to accept yourself conditionally (because you believe in a grace-giving god or son-of-god), *you* choose to believe in this religion and you consequently create the grace-giver who "makes" you self-acceptable.[47] (Italics his.)

It is amazing that Christians choose to drink from such anti-Christian psychological belief systems.

In *Effective Biblical Counseling*, Crabb lists a number of psychologists and recommends their books. The following summary statement from the end of his chapter

"Christianity and Psychology" illustrates Crabb's confidence in psychology. All names in the parentheses are in his original statement.

> Man is responsible (Glasser) to believe truth which will result in responsible behavior (Ellis) that will provide him with meaning, hope (Frankl), and love (Fromm) and will serve as a guide (Adler) to effective living with others as a self- and other-accepting person (Harris), who understands himself (Freud), who appropriately expresses himself (Perls), and who knows how to control himself (Skinner).[48]

But Glasser's responsibility has nothing to do with God or His measure of right and wrong; Ellis equates godlessness with mental health; the hope that Frankl gives is not a sure hope because it is man-centered; the love of Fromm is a far cry from the love that Jesus teaches and gives; Adler's guide is self rather than God; Harris's acceptance disregards God's law; Freud hardly understood himself and he repudiated God; Perls' expression focuses on feelings and self; and Skinner's methods of self-control work better with animals than humans. Why not give credit where credit is due? To the Lord and His Word! **Why not look to God's Word concerning responsibility, truth, meaning, hope, love, guidance for effective living, understanding oneself, expression, and self-control instead of rummaging around in the broken cisterns of the opinions of unredeemed men?**

6

The Unconscious: A Key to Understanding?

For Freudians, the unconscious mind provides the magic key that unlocks the true knowledge of the person. The notion of a magic key grows out of their opinion that the unconscious directs and motivates behavior. Hence, if you desire to understand people, you must deal first and foremost with the unconscious. Only in this way can one unravel the "tangled web" of bizarre and troubling behavior.

One does not have to follow all of Freud's theories to be identified as a Freudian. An article in *Scientific American* titled "Why Freud Isn't Dead" explains that specific Freudian ideas, such as the Oedipus Complex, have "fallen out of favor even among psychoanalysts," but that they continue to hold onto Freud's idea of a powerful motivating unconscious. Morris Eagle, president of the psychoanalysis division of the American Psychological Association and a professor at Adelphi University says, "There are very few analysts who follow all of Freud's formulations." The *Scientific American* article goes on to state:

> Nevertheless, psychotherapists of all stripes still tend to share two of Freud's core beliefs: One is that our behavior, thoughts and emotions stem from unconscious fears and desires, often rooted in childhood experiences. The other is that with the help of a trained therapist, we can understand the source of our troubles and thereby obtain some relief.[1]

Likewise, Crabb does not follow all of Freud's formulations, but the above quote describes his commitment to the Freudian unconscious.

Crabb has said of us, "Their major critique of me seems to be that I hold to a Freudian unconscious (which I simply don't)."[2] It is sad that Crabb, who is trained as a psychologist does not know that one does not have to accept the Freudian Oedipus Complex in order to "hold to a Freudian unconscious." Based on what he teaches, Crabb will be labeled as a Freudian by anyone who truly knows both Freud's and Crabb's teachings. This we demonstrate throughout this book.

Crabb suggests that Christian counselors cannot hope to properly analyze and counsel people unless they also understand and analyze the unconscious.[3] He clearly states that each of us has been programmed in the unconscious mind.[4] He teaches that thoughts and evaluations made at the conscious level are powerfully influenced by the unconscious:

The sentences we consciously tell ourselves strongly influence how we feel and what we do. We now can see where these sentences originate. The content of the sentences we tell ourselves in our conscious minds draws upon the wrong assumptions held by our unconscious minds.[5]

While Crabb believes this to be true, there is no evidence to support his assumption that people's wrong assumptions or sentences said to themselves originate in this type of Freudian-based unconscious.

Nevertheless, Crabb contends that conscious activity is constantly motivated by the content of the unconscious in a powerful and pervasive manner. He says:

> Though we may not be consciously aware of what we are telling ourselves at every given moment, the words that fill our minds control much of what we do and feel. Much of our behavior is a direct product of what we are thinking **unconsciously**.[6] (Bold added.)

> Not only the motives but also the unique theme or style of our interactions remains unidentified. . . .[7]

> Therefore the sinfully wrong strategies by which we manipulate people with our well-being in mind are intentionally hidden from view. They take their place in the **unconscious**.[8] (Bold added.)

Belief that unconscious thinking controls and determines behavior not only saturates his books; each case history that Crabb interprets inevitably reveals unconscious assumptions and beliefs **controlling** conscious activity. For example, he says:

Consider what happens as a girl watches her mother cry because her daddy doesn't come home at night. This unfortunate girl may learn the belief that men hurt women. She may then (**unconsciously**) set for herself the goal of never becoming emotionally vulnerable to a man. When she marries, her goal will motivate her to keep her distance, never to relax in her husband's love, never to give herself freely to him.[9] (Bold added.)

Psychologists cannot predict behavior. But when a person has problems later in life, a psychologist may try to find out what happened earlier and then apply his theories to explain what happened and why. If behavior cannot be predicted, as Freud readily admitted, such understanding is only guess-work.

Crabb believes that this woman's conduct as a wife and mother is controlled by past events and unconscious beliefs motivating her from her unconscious. According to this system it is impossible for a person to change without discovering and confronting those so-called unconscious thought-patterns. He contends that *"if no work is done beneath the water line, then work above the water line results in a disastrous externalism."*[10] (Italics his.) Remember that "below the water line" represents the unconscious. Crabb goes on to say that the unconscious contents truly determine the way in which people live. He says:

We must learn to deal with problems below the water line that typically remain unidentified but still have serious effects on how we live. . . . There are, I believe, processes going on within our personalities that **determine** the directions we move. . . .[11] (Bold added.)

The Unconscious:
Scientific Fact or Fiction?

Crabb speaks of his Freudian-based theory of the unconscious as though it were a scientifically established fact. But it is mere opinion. No one has ever proven that the Freudian unconscious exists. Nor has anyone scientifically verified the contents of the unconscious.

Just because psychological systems and personality theories **seem** to explain the person and his behavior, that does not mean the explanations are accurate. When we consider that there are numerous competing systems, each of which pretends to explain personhood, something must be amiss. World-renowned scholar and philosopher of science Sir Karl Popper examined these psychological theories. He says:

> These theories appeared to be able to explain practically everything that happened within the fields to which they referred. The study of any of them seemed to have the effect of an intellectual conversion or revelation, opening your eyes to a new truth hidden from those not yet initiated. Once your eyes were thus opened you saw confirming instances everywhere: the world was full of *verifications* of the theory. Whatever happened always confirmed it.[12] (Emphasis his.)

At first glance this looks like promising evidence. However, Popper insists that constant confirmations and seeming ability to explain everything do not indicate scientific validity. What looks like a strength is actually a weakness. He says:

> It is easy to obtain confirmations or verifications, for nearly every theory—if we look for confirmations. . .. Confirming evidence should not count *except when it is the result of a genuine test of the theory.*[13] (Emphasis his.)

He also indicates that psychological theories such as Freud's and others' do not meet scientific requirements:

> A theory which is not refutable by any conceivable event is nonscientific. Irrefutability is not a virtue of a theory (as people often think) but a vice.[14]

He concludes that "though posing as sciences," such theories "had in fact more in common with primitive myths than with science; that they resembled astrology rather than astronomy."[15]

One can interpret the same feeling or behavior in a great variety of ways. But that is all it is, speculation and interpretation. One can even impose psychological interpretations on the Bible, but the interpretations distort the true meaning of Scripture. And then, with a particular psychological interpretation, the Bible can appear to verify that same psychological system. This can be done by nearly every psychological system and theory, including the theory of the unconscious.

The Freudian unconscious as the key element in understanding and solving problems is based upon pure conjecture. Popper is not the only one who has compared such theories with astrology. Researcher Carol Tavris says:

> Now the irony is that many people who are not fooled by astrology for one minute subject them-

selves to therapy for years, where the same error of logic and interpretation often occur.[16]

Another researcher also refers to such psychological theories as myths because "they are not subject to disproof."[17] **Anyone can devise a system of explaining human nature and behavior and then interpret all behavior in light of his explanation.** This is true not only of theories of the unconscious; it is true for graphology, astrology, phrenology, palm reading, and a host of other questionable practices.

Crabb's readers could conclude that his integration material on the unconscious is beyond dispute. Yet Crabb never gives scientific support for the concept. The existence and contents of the Freudian unconscious and Crabb's adaptation of the Freudian unconscious have never been proven. Nevertheless the idea of the unconscious so pervades our society and the church that nearly everyone takes it for granted.

Commitment to the Unconscious

Although there is no biblical or scientific proof for the existence of the Freudian unconscious, Crabb structures his entire system on the rudiments of this Freudian fabrication. He declares, "There is an unconscious."[18] Then instead of supporting his statement with evidence to prove that there is an unconscious that powerfully directs and motivates all behavior, he makes this general statement about awareness: "We are simply not aware of all that we are doing in our deceitful hearts."[19] However, this general observation does not support Crabb's elaborate psychological theory of the unconscious. Then as a further attempt to assert the existence of the unconscious, he declares, "And *we don't want* to be aware of what we really believe and the direction we in fact are moving."[20] (Italics his.) This statement implies an across-the-board application to all Christians. But, there are many who are aware of what they believe and are desiring to be:

> . . . filled with the knowledge of his will in all wisdom and spiritual understanding; that [they] might walk worthy of the Lord unto all pleasing, being fruitful in every good work, and increasing in the knowledge of God; strengthened with all might, according to his glorious power, unto all patience and longsuffering with joyfulness; giving thanks unto the Father, which hath made [them] meet to be partakers of the inheritance of the saints in light. (Colossians 1:9-11.)

Crabb not only insists on the existence of the unconscious, but on the necessity of a counselor or other initiate to expose the contents of the unconscious. He says, *"It is therefore true that no one sees himself clearly until he is exposed by another."*[21] (Italics his.) This denies the sovereign work of God in a person's life. The Word of God places itself as the mirror to expose sin and the Holy Spirit enables a person to see his error and correct it. While there are times when the Lord uses another believer, that is not the usual manner. And one must be careful about exposing another. One can confront another's external sin, but only God can see inside a person, know his thoughts and motives, and expose internal sin.

The unconscious is the cornerstone of Crabb's counseling model. He reveals firm commitment to psychological theories of the unconscious throughout his writing. In *Inside Out* he uses such terms as *inside, underground* , and *beneath the surface*, rather than the word *unconscious*.[22] His oft-stated notion that real change requires an inside look[23] or looking "beneath the surface"[24] is none other than a veiled reference to the unconscious. His "inside" theme points to the same personality theory contained in *Understanding People*, in which he emphasizes the centrality of the unconscious as the key to understanding and change.[25] When he proclaims the necessity of looking at the "deepest parts of the soul," or of a deep "inward look," he is clearly referring to a psychoanalytic theory of the unconscious.

Are Theories of the Unconscious in the Bible?

Although a Freudian-based theory of the unconscious serves as the foundation of Crabb's system, his books do not give adequate biblical support for such a centralized and dominant emphasis. In his books are lengthy discussions on such things as unconscious motivational factors, the contents of the unconscious, and how to change unconscious beliefs, but little attempt to verify those discussions from the Scriptures.

In *Effective Biblical Counseling* Crabb offers his definition of the unconscious to be "*the reservoir of basic assumptions which people firmly and emotionally hold about how to meet their needs of significance and security.*"[26] (Emphasis his.) The same general definition can be found in psychology textbooks. The supposed scriptural warrant for Crabb's definition and for his entire presentation on the unconscious is a study he did on the New Testament Greek term *phronema*, which is translated *mind*. He says:

> I recently listed every verse in which this word (or a
> derivative) is used. From my study of these pas-
> sages, it appears that the central concept expressed
> by the word is a part of personality which develops
> and holds on to deep, reflective assumptions. . . . Let
> me tentatively suggest that this concept corresponds
> closely to what psychologists call the "unconscious
> mind."[27]

It looks like Crabb was looking for biblical confirmation
for the existence of "what psychologists call the 'unconscious mind.'"

Crabb himself is so uncertain of the results of his
study, that he can only "tentatively suggest" that it con-
firms his detailed discussion of the unconscious. We must
have more certainty than that, especially when presenting a view of personality that is supposed to be consistent
with Scripture.[28] Indeed, Crabb's seeming hesitation
about the results of his word study is well founded. The
New Testament Greek term *phronema* does not refer to
the notions presented in Crabb's discussion of the unconscious. His description of the unconscious as the reservoir
of basic assumptions about how to satisfy our two deepest
needs is not implied by the term *phronema*.

Phronema and the verb form *phroneo* refer strictly to
conscious thought processes. According to Vine's dictionary, *phronema* refers to what a person has in mind, the
thought, or the object of thought. *Phroneo* means "to
think, to be minded in a certain way. . . to think of, to be
mindful of."

Phroneo has to do with "moral interest or reflection,
not mere unreasoning opinion."[29] There is no hint in the
immediate context or in the biblical use of the Greek
word that it corresponds to the psychological version of
the unconscious or unconscious thought. Every usage in

the New Testament refers to conscious thought processes, that is, to rationally controlled thought at the conscious level. One could search both ancient and modern lexicons and Bible dictionaries and not find anyone define *phronema* as the reservoir of unconscious assumptions about how to meet two particular needs.

Continuing his search for biblical support for his theories on the unconscious, Crabb quotes Romans 12:1-2.

> I beseech you therefore, brethren, by the mercies of God, that ye present your bodies a living sacrifice, holy, acceptable unto God, which is your reasonable service. And be not conformed to this world: but be ye transformed by the renewing of your mind, that ye may prove what is that good, and acceptable, and perfect, will of God.

Crabb uses this as biblical proof for unconscious beliefs and motives.[30] He uses the phrase "renewing the mind" as a direct parallel to his theory of dealing with the unconscious throughout his books.[31] Nevertheless Romans 12:2 will not support Crabb's notions of the unconscious. The renewing of the mind has to do with the rest of Romans 12. Paul is speaking of conscious thinking, such as:

> For I say, through the grace given unto me, to every man that is among you, not to think of himself more highly than he ought to think; but to think soberly, according as God hath dealt to every man the measure of faith. (Romans 12:3.)

Paul then goes on to explain the operation of each member in the body of Christ. He continues with admonitions to "love without dissimulation," to "abhor that which is

evil," to "cleave to that which is good," to be "kindly affec-
tioned one to another with brotherly love," not to be
"slothful in business," to be "fervent in spirit," to serve the
Lord, to rejoice in hope, to be patient in tribulation, to
distribute to the needy, to exercise hospitality, and so
forth (Romans 12:4-21.) Paul is talking about consciously
thinking about things differently from the way the world
thinks. He is talking about conscious attitudes, conscious
choices, and conscious thoughts behind conscious actions
being changed, because of the new life in Jesus. Finding
the unconscious with deep needs, strategies, and pain in
Romans 12:2 requires a very imaginative handling of the
text.

If insight into the unconscious is central to understanding people, God would have made it central to His
doctrine of man. However, such a doctrine had not been
discovered throughout the centuries. It seems a bit odd
that such a crucial doctrine would have been hidden all
these years and now only be discovered through the help
of minds that are darkened to the Word of God. Even now,
with the invention of the so-called unconscious, one must
distort Scripture to make it fit.

In addition to superimposing his notions of the unconscious upon the biblical term translated *mind*, Crabb
seeks to equate the word *heart* with the unconscious:

> My understanding of unconscious elements within
> the personality is rooted in the biblical teaching
> that, above all else, our hearts are deceitful and des-
> perately wicked.[32]

According to God's revelation the heart is deceitful. However, the deceitfulness of a person's inner being does not
prove or even imply that a person's heart or inner being
is the unconscious described by Crabb. The word *heart* as

employed in Scripture will not support his psychological agenda concerning the unconscious, its crucial role, or its contents.

The doctrine of the unconscious is an entire ideology existing independent from and contradictory to what Scripture teaches about the human condition. It subverts clear biblical teaching on the nature of man. It alters the focus of sanctification from the way of the cross to the psychological notion of exposing the unconscious. It reduces the spiritual work of the Holy Spirit in the inner man to a psychological work in the unconscious. And, the supernatural transformation of the inner man is replaced by a human method of changing oneself through an altered perception of how so-called needs are met.

The Bible stresses the glorious presence and power of the Holy Spirit in the inner man. Thus, we would pray with Paul:

> Of whom the whole family in heaven and earth is named, that he would grant you, according to the riches of his glory, to be strengthened with might by his Spirit in the inner man; that Christ may dwell in your hearts by faith; that ye, being rooted and grounded in love, may be able to comprehend with all saints what is the breadth, and length, and depth, and height; And to know the love of Christ, which passeth knowledge, that ye might be filled with all the fulness of God. Now unto him that is able to do exceeding abundantly above all that we ask or think, according to the power that worketh in us, unto him be glory in the church by Christ Jesus throughout all ages, world without end. Amen. (Ephesians 3:15-21.)

Belief in the Freudian unconscious harmonizes with Hinduism rather than with Christianity. In his book *The Religions of Man*, Houston Smith says, "The Hindu concept of man rests on the basic thesis that he is a layered being."[33] He says:

> Hinduism agrees with psychoanalysis [Freud] that if only we could dredge up a portion of our lost individual totality—the third part of our being [the unconscious]—we would experience a remarkable expansion of our powers, a vivid refreshening of life.[34]

Just as in psychoanalysis, Hindus believe that the unconscious contains both yearnings (drives) and suppressions (ego-defense mechanisms). We say this to illustrate the fact that any attempt to understand the thoughts and intents of the heart and the why's and wherefore's of human behavior is a religious exercise. The religion may be psychoanalytic, humanistic, transpersonal, Moslem, Hindu, or Christian. However if a Christian dips into the cisterns of psychological opinions, he cannot be offering the pure water of the truth of God.

7

Need-Driven Theology

Crabb's model of counseling centers on the belief that unconscious needs direct and motivate behavior. He declares, "In order to understand biblical counseling, we must identify clearly the deepest personal needs of people."[1] When he speaks of "deepest personal needs" he is referring to a need for worthwhileness which he divides into needs for security and significance.[2] In his later books he refers to those needs as deep longings for relationship and impact. In his latest books he refers to deep longings for relationship, connection, and releasing capacities of goodness.

Examining the concept of personal needs can be somewhat confusing because of the chameleon-like nature of the very term itself. The term *needs* can take on a variety

129

of meanings according to the purpose of the person employing it. For example someone will say, "What do you need (want)?" A Christian will speak of the need for a Savior. Ministers speak of meeting the needs of their people in terms of shepherding them and nourishing them in the Word. Thus it is necessary to examine Crabb's concept of needs.

Crabb presents the unconscious as a powerful reality submerged beneath the conscious mind. He places great importance on the contents of the unconscious in terms of the way they affect all of behavior. They include personal needs of security and significance,[3] basic assumptions on how to meet those needs,[4] "relational pain" and "relational strategies."[5]

In *Inside Out* Crabb uses the terms *deep longings*, *thirst* and *wrong strategies* to describe the unconscious—its contents, power, and influence.[6] In *Finding God* he calls these "thirst-driven passions."[7]

Powerful Needs in the Unconscious

A foundational proposition in Crabb's system is that **every person has two substantive needs in the unconscious which motivate behavior.** He later substitutes the word *needs* with *longings* and *passions* and the word *unconscious* with *core* and *soul*. That this concept is central to Crabb's model is obvious just by skimming the contents of his books.

According to Crabb, unmet needs produce loneliness, sorrow, and intense pain. Therefore, counseling people into an awareness of their unconscious needs and strategies is difficult. Because of the "intense pain" of unmet needs and because of the "excruciating hurt" from the failure of their unconscious strategies, people build "self-protective" layers to insulate themselves against further injury.

According to Crabb, those self-protective layers cause people to deny the reality of their true goals and motives. Through the process of denial, people supposedly develop layers to insulate themselves from painful unconscious realities and to obstruct attempts to expose their true motives. Although strategies of self-protection manifest themselves at the conscious level, people supposedly do not consciously know that what they are doing is for the purpose of self-protection. Crabb uses the distinction between the two levels of the mind to infer that while people may appear happy on the surface, there is a huge possibility that they are really miserable and lonely inside.

Crabb gives an example of a man he calls Frank, who is highly motivated and successful. Frank's conscious overt activities include business success, a lovely wife and home, three intelligent children, and positive church experiences. In fact, Frank "feels really good about life and shares with passion the joys of living for Jesus."[8] But Crabb contends that what is seen on the surface does not reveal the true source of Frank's motives. According to Crabb, Frank's "upbeat, assertive, knowledgeable" manner which leads to outward success and an outward life "above reproach and worthy of respect" is actually his way to protect himself "from ever having to admit he can't resolve a problem." Crabb contends that beneath Frank's outward joy and life of accomplishment there is a desperately fearful man "longing for a level of respectful involvement he's never enjoyed" and a sense of painful inadequacy.[9] Therefore this man, like all others, is supposedly unaware of his pain and seeks to protect himself through Freudian ego-defense mechanisms of unconscious repression and denial. In other words, the man in his unconscious life is the opposite of the man in his conscious life.

Counseling according to Crabb's theory then must be a process of exposing unconscious pain and self-protective strategies. The counselor must strip away defensive layers to expose the confused world of the unconscious. Once the layers have been peeled away, pains and hurts of the unconscious can be exposed. Crabb considers approaches which do not peel the layers to be superficial and simplistic.

According to Crabb's system, unmet needs, wrong strategies about satisfying them, pain and hurt of failure, and so forth must be unearthed and faced honestly even though the process can be excruciating. He contends that real change is only possible if a person is willing to start from the inside, meaning the unconscious.

After unconscious causes of the problems have been exposed, the counselor can set about the process of reprogramming both the conscious mind and the unconscious. This is accomplished through a focused effort to program into the mind a new strategy about how to satisfy the two needs. Again this is not an easy task. The person must jump from the cliff of safety and trust God to meet his two needs in the unconscious. Only then, according to Crabb, can he learn to depend both consciously and unconsciously on God. In Crabb's later writings he goes beyond exposing the negative contents of the unconscious and proposes ways of exposing and releasing hidden gems.

Crabb's Model of Four Circles

Crabb devised a "four-circle model of personality," in which the unconscious plays the dominant role.[10] His four circles are: Personal, Rational, Volitional, and

Emotional. Each circle represents different aspects of the individual as he relates to life through conscious and unconscious activity.

Personal Circle. Crabb says the Personal Circle is a person's "Capacity for Relationship and Impact."[11] He identifies this capacity as a God-created need. He says,

> *The basic personal need of each personal being is to regard himself as a worthwhile human being.*[12] (Italics his.)

According to Crabb, the need to be worthwhile has two components: the need for security and the need for significance, or deep longings for relationship and impact, and later on as passions for connecting and releasing hidden capacities. He theorizes that the deep longings are related to a relentless fear of rejection, of not being acceptable, of not being of value or significance. In fact, Crabb teaches that the primary motivating force in every person is fear of not being accepted, of not being secure and significant. And the goal of behavior is to be accepted as worthwhile, with security and significance.[13] In his later work acceptance through connecting is extolled as the way to expose the bad and release the good.

In Crabb's model the Personal Circle of powerful needs is the core of every person, and it is primarily unconscious. Thus, even though a person may be superficially aware of having those needs, their power and thrust come from the unconscious. From this hidden, nearly inaccessible realm, these needs motivate everything a person does. Crabb compares the needs for significance and security with Freud's drives for power and pleasure.[14] We also see the influence of Adler, Maslow, and Rogers in Crabb's Personal Circle.

Rational Circle. The key feature of the Rational Circle is its unconscious beliefs and strategies about how to meet the needs for security and significance (deep longings for relationship and impact). While the Rational Circle includes all mental processes, such as thoughts, concepts, beliefs, and images,[15] the emphasis is on so-called unconscious beliefs and motives.[16] Thus the Rational Circle largely works from the unconscious to satisfy the so-called needs of the Personal Circle. Crabb contends that unconscious denial, erroneous thinking, wrong conclusions, and wrong beliefs in the Rational Circle need to be replaced with accurate thinking so that needs for security/relationship and significance/impact can be met more effectively.[17] The influence of Freud, Adler, Maslow and Ellis can be seen in Crabb's Rational Circle.

Volitional Circle. Crabb's Volitional Circle represents a person's choosing capacity.[18] He says that people choose their behavior and are therefore responsible. Yet, according to his system, a great deal of choice in terms of strategies and goals is based upon the unconscious assumptions, beliefs, and strategies of the Rational Circle about how to meet the demands of the needs/longings in the Personal Circle. Although the Volitional Circle largely represents conscious activity, it operates according to the needs and dictates of the unconscious.[19] Crabb's Volitional Circle shows the influence of Freud, Adler, Ellis, and Glasser.

The Emotional Circle. The Emotional Circle is where counselees experience feeling. They are encouraged to get in touch with their feelings, since the really deep emotions exert their power from the unconscious. According to Crabb's system, emotional experiences, whether pleasant or unpleasant, relate directly to success in satisfying the demands of the needs/longings. Certain emotions are triggered by the vast array of unconscious beliefs and thoughts about how to satisfy the two needs. Thus emotions play a key role in exposing the unconscious. The idea is that if a person can experience those emotions in his conscious awareness, he may be able to penetrate the contents of his unconscious. Then by bringing more and more material into the conscious realm, he will be able to think more accurately, choose with greater awareness, and develop more effective strategies for meeting his unconscious needs.[20] The influence of Freud, Adler, Rogers, and Perls is evident in Crabb's Emotional Circle.

Changes in Vocabulary and Emphasis

Crabb's changes in vocabulary and emphasis do not indicate substantial change in his underlying theory of personality. In his earlier books Crabb calls the two unconscious needs "security" and "significance." Later he changes his terminology to "longings" for "relationship and impact" and "passion" for "connecting" and "releasing capacities." However, as Crabb himself indicates, his change in words does not involve any change in the doctrine. He says:

> Readers familiar with my earlier books will recognize movement in my concepts but not, I think, fundamental change. For example, my preference now is to speak of *deep longings in the human heart for relationship and impact* rather than *personal needs for security and significance.*[21] (Emphasis his)

Here Crabb affirms that personal needs and deep longings identify the same doctrine of man in his system.

The following is Crabb's description of the needs and their location:

> **Deep inside** each of these people rumbled a **persistent demand**, one which they **couldn't clearly hear** themselves saying, yet one which was **driving them ruthlessly in disastrous directions**. If we could listen to the **faint but powerful murmurings** of their **unconscious minds** we would hear something like this: I **need** to respect myself as a worthwhile person. . . . Sorting through this "stream of unconsciousness" a simple organization emerges: people have one basic personal **need which requires** two kinds of input for its satisfaction. The most basic **need** is a sense of **personal worth**, an acceptance of oneself as a whole, real person. The two required inputs are *significance . . . and security*.[22] (Italics his; bold added.)

Thus the needs for security and significance are ruthless drives in the unconscious. As he says in *Inside Out,* "The consequence of living with no satisfaction of our crucial longings is the beginning of hell."[23]

Crabb even assigns an independent existence to the two needs. He says:

> The intangible identity that I know as "Me" has **two real and profound needs**, which are **substantive personal realities** not reducible to biological or chemical analysis. They have a **personal existence, independent of the physical body**, that constitutes the core of what it means to be a spirit.[24] (Bold added.)

Not only are they "substantive personal realities"; they constitute "the core of what it means to be a spirit." Thus in Crabb's system the two needs constitute the essence of personhood. He says:

The need to regard oneself as worthwhile by experiencing significance and security is unalterably a part of the human personality.[25]
(Bold added.)

However, the Bible points to a different picture of mankind. Rather than being driven by the need for worthwhileness experienced as needs for security and significance (or relationship and impact or connection and release), the Bible teaches that humans are driven by the sinful self. The problem is self at the center as an insatiable, rebellious tyrant. Since the Fall, man has required a Savior from sin, not a satisfier of powerful unconscious needs driving behavior outside a person's awareness. Instead of so-called unconscious needs being met, the power of sin must be broken. The domination of sin is so great that a person must be born of the Spirit, regenerated by the very life of God. This work of God is never described in the Bible as the satisfaction of unconscious needs crying out for security and significance. The separation of man from God through sin is so vast that a person cannot repair the breach by engaging in Crabb's techniques of realizing inner pain thereby finding God and discovering that God can meet unconscious needs. In fact, it is only by God's grace that a person even realizes that he is undone by sin. Only by God's grace does a person exercise the kind of faith that enables him to walk in the Spirit, with an obedient heart that desires to please God rather than self.

The Bible says that a sinner's inclination is rebellion against rather than yearning for God. Therefore, the needs that Crabb identifies with all people cannot be equated with yearning for God in the biblical sense. The very nature of sin is to be one's own little god rather than submitting to Christ. Before a person is made new through Christ, the essence of his personhood is the sinful self. After regeneration, it is the Holy Spirit enabling him to know, love, and serve God. The Bible, not psychology, is God's revelation concerning the essence of man before and after salvation.

Need Psychology/ Theology

Crabb's model may sound good on the surface. After all, who has not felt the stirrings of the soul longing for satisfaction? His emphasis on personal needs and longings finds eager reception in the church. His plea for meaningful intimate relationships with God and with fellow believers causes people to be hopeful about his methods. And the implied promises for love, purpose, and meaning saturate the pages of his books. However, Crabb's doctrine of man with unconscious needs motivating all behavior is psychologically based. And his doctrine of change, with unconscious beliefs and strategies for meeting the needs, is also grounded in psychological ideas. His exposure of needs, including capacities to be released, continues throughout his books.

Crabb's model borrows significantly from humanistic psychology. Humanistic psychology is based on the belief that people are born good and that society (especially parents) corrupts them. Humanistic psychologists further believe that certain needs motivate everything a person does, that a person's life plan is to fulfill those inborn, unmet needs, and that when those needs are met the person will be able to realize his full potential and be socially responsible. They identify those psychological needs with such words as: *self-esteem*, *worthwhileness*, *emotional security*, and *significance*.

Their hope for mankind is this: when individual psychological needs are met then people will be personally fulfilled and socially responsible. They will be loving, peaceful, creative, industrious, and unselfish. They will no longer try to fill their emptiness (unfulfilled needs) with alcohol, drugs, or any other kind of overindulgence. In short, according to their theories, if everyone were to reach self-actualization (all needs being met) we would have a utopian society.

Many Christians have bought into the humanistic lie that when people's needs are met, they will be good, loving people. Through the influence of humanistic psychology, they believe that people sin because their needs are not met. Some say that teenagers rebel because their needs have not been met. They contend that failure to live the Christian life is because Christians do not have enough self-esteem or they do not understand that all of those so-called psychological needs are met in Christ. They reduce the Gospel to the good news of personal worth, emotional security, significance, and unrealized goodness. And they believe that if only Christians would see that God meets all of those needs they will be able to live the Christian life effectively.

Scripture, however, does not bear this out. Adam and Eve had it all. There was no need in their lives that was not being met to its very fullest, and yet they chose to sin, have their own way, disbelieve God, believe a lie, and love self more than to love and obey God. They followed both the words and example of Satan, who as Lucifer had it all: beauty, power, authority, love, and all that an archangel could have and be. But Lucifer wanted to be God. And what about Israel? The more their needs were met, the less they relied on God. The more their needs were met, the more sinful they became. Even the fulfilling of legitimate needs will not make a person a saint or promote sanctification.

And here we must delineate between true human need, according to the Bible, and what humanistic psychologists place at the center of human need. The Bible places God's will and purpose at the center rather than so-called psychological need. In His gracious will Jesus gives of Himself, not according to what psychologists identify as essential personal needs, but according to His perfect love and intimate knowledge of each person.

Throughout the Bible the panorama of God's plan for humanity unfolds according to His own will and purpose, which includes, but goes far beyond, human need. But since those psychological theories were devised by people who were seeking to understand themselves and humanity apart from God and who were looking for solutions separated from the sovereignty and will of God, their central interest was what they believed to be human need and human fulfillment without God.

Because humanistic psychology is based on humanism rather than theism, it ignores longings for worship, godly righteousness, discipline, faith in God, spiritual truth, pleasing God, loving God, obeying God, and other intricacies that God knows about each person. Instead, all is centered in the self. And when Christians try to amalgamate humanistic psychology with the Bible, they tend to ignore, distort, or subsume all spiritual blessings under what they call psychological needs.

The idea that humans are motivated by powerful needs in the unconscious is an unproven assumption that many Christians have come to believe. In fact, people do not think twice when someone says that people are motivated by inner needs. Tony Walter, in his book *Need: The New Religion*, says:

> It is fashionable to follow the view of some psychologists that the self is a bundle of needs and that per-

sonal growth is the business of progressively meeting these needs. Many Christians go along with such beliefs.[26]

Walter also contends that needs now constitute a new morality and says:

> One mark of the almost total success of this new morality is that the Christian Church, traditionally keen on mortifying the desires of the flesh, on crucifying the needs of the self in pursuit of the religious life, has eagerly adopted the language of needs for itself. . . we now hear that "Jesus will meet your every need," as though he were some kind of divine psychiatrist or divine detergent, as though God were simply to service us.[27]

But Walter further declares that "human need was never central to Christian theology. What was central was God's grace not human need. Christianity is at root God-centered, not man-centered."[28]

Psychological systems, however, are man-centered and were proposed as alternative means of understanding the human condition and wrestling with problems of living. God's law was replaced by humanistic values which turned into needs, which gave them a moral force. Abraham Maslow built his hierarchy of needs on his own beliefs and values. And since he placed a high value on self-worth, self-esteem, and self-actualization, he justified those values by turning them into needs. And while humanistic psychologists have removed the *ought's* and *should's* of external moral codes (such as the Bible), they have presented their own morality of needs. Walter notes:

> . . . the human project as the progressive meeting of
> human need has been unmasked; it is a secular reli-
> gion, or at least a secular morality. I suggest that
> atheists and agnostics who pride themselves on
> having dispensed with morality and religion should
> ponder whether they have not let both in again
> through the back door.[29]

Indeed, need psychology has the force of morality and the
power of religion. And Walter identifies this new morality
and new religion as **not** compatible with Christianity. He
says:

> There is one feature of some of the major writings
> on need that points towards need as a form of
> morality. Marx, Fromm, Maslow and others have
> noted the incompatibility between human beings
> orienting their lives to meeting their needs, and a
> traditional Christianity that would deny the needs
> of the self and would give charity to others not
> because their needs entitled them to it but out of
> sheer disinterested love. . . . Life as a project of
> meeting needs becomes almost a substitute,
> disguised religion.[30]

Nevertheless, Crabb attempts to combine need
psychology with the Bible. He makes the needs of men
appear synonymous with God's will and purpose.[31] He
equates those needs with God-given capacities.[32] Thus in
his system it follows that the underlying need to be
worthwhile is a God-given capacity. He relates the need
for significance (also called "impact") with the capacity to
fulfill God's purposes and the need for security (also
called "relationship") with the God-given capacity for
relationship with God. In his attempts to join together

man-centered psychological theories with the Bible, Crabb has created a "Need Theology."

Need theology turns everything around. Not only does the human take center stage, but his so-called psychological needs are of prime importance. In Crabb's system the contents of the unconscious direct, motivate, and energize every aspect of a person's life. Those needs are not regarded as something negative, but rather as positive capacities to be filled. **This is an unknown view of the innermost nature of man in the long annals of church history.**

Because of the centrality and the legitimacy of the needs in Crabb's theology, they play an essential role in his doctrine of sin. In his system sin is defined as the attempt to fulfill the demands of those unconscious needs apart from God. However, according to the Bible the sin problem is much deeper than strategies for meeting those unconscious needs apart from God. The Bible reveals something quite different about the human heart and its sinfulness. Paul likened the condition of the unredeemed sinner as "dead in trespasses and sins" and "children of disobedience: among whom also we all had our conversation in times past in the lusts of our flesh, fulfilling the desires of the flesh and of the mind, and were by nature the children of wrath" (Ephesians 2:1,3). Nowhere in Scripture is the doctrine of sin interpreted in light of supposed strategies about satisfying two unconscious needs.

In Crabb's doctrine of salvation, the way of the cross turns into a message of escape from the tyranny of unmet needs. Both regeneration and sanctification are reinterpreted in light of unconscious needs and unreleased capacities. Thus real change according to Need Theology is learning how to meet the demands of needs/longings/passions with God's help rather than independently. However, Jesus did not die on the cross to satisfy a supposed need for worth, but to redeem human beings from the clutches of sin and Satan. He changes their lives from the inside without psychospiritual processing. He does not merely alter thinking driven by unconscious need fulfillment; he changes the very desires of the heart. Christ changes believers' motivation to love for God and others. Paul tells about this wonderful, life-transforming change: "Therefore if any man be in Christ he is a new creature: old things are passed away; behold all things are become new" (2 Corinthians 5:17).

The way of sanctification through Need Theology is to explore the caverns of the unconscious where the needs reside, to uncover the pain of unmet needs, and thereby to become dependent on God. In *Connecting* Crabb adds spelunking for gems of goodness that need to be exposed.

Although a Christian is to examine himself in the light of God's Word to see that he is walking in the Spirit, biblical sanctification is quite different from concentrating on unmet needs, feeling the pain of the past, and then learning about God meeting those needs. According to the Bible, the focus of the vision of the believer is drawn from self to Christ through the Holy Spirit and the Word of God. Believers become more like Him as they look at Him and to Him:

> But we all, with open face beholding as in a glass the glory of the Lord, are changed into the same image from glory to glory, even as by the Spirit of the Lord. (2 Corinthians 3:18.)

It is by looking at Jesus, not at themselves, that believers take on His character through the gracious work of the Holy Spirit. Furthermore, sanctification calls for taking up one's cross, not taking up new strategies for need fulfillment.

Although Crabb objects to criticism about his teachings having "a man-centered focus on fulfillment rather than a God-centered emphasis on obedience to Him and preoccupation with His Glory,"[33] what he teaches does indeed lead to a humanistic rather than a godly emphasis. The reason why this happens is because Crabb's integration includes the doctrines of men whose psychologies center on man and his innate goodness, his worthwhileness, his psychological reasons for behavior, and his goal of fulfillment.

No matter how much Crabb desires his system to free people to love and serve God and to relate warmly with people, the focus on human need will counteract his goal. The Bible calls believers to walk by faith rather than by any needs or desires of the self-life. Crabb encourages people to focus on themselves so that they can become better Christians.

Jesus set the tone of the Christian way by His life and doctrine. Paul urges us to follow after His excellent example of self-denial in Philippians 2:2-8. Indeed the Lord Himself set the denial of self as a fundamental requirement of Christian discipleship:

> If any man will come after me, let him deny himself, and take up his cross, and follow me. For whosoever will save his life shall lose it: and whosoever will lose his life for my sake shall find it. (Matthew 16:24-25.)

Denying self is quite the opposite from seeking to satisfy self. Maslow's system and all of the humanistic, psychoanalytic, behavioristic, and transpersonal psychologies have set out to oppose and destroy the way of the Cross.

How can Christians hope to successfully incorporate such psychological viewpoints into the biblical way of life?

8

Unconscious Motivators of Behavior

Crabb's clearest presentation of unconscious motivation is in his propositions on motivation in *Effective Biblical Counseling.*[1] Although in later books he shifts from his five propositions on motivation to a four-fold explanation of the image of God, the doctrine remains the same.[2] Crabb's secularly-derived explanation of motivation almost sounds biblical when he discusses it in terms of the image of God. But, the shift in terminology does not reflect a shift in doctrinal content. Crabb sees man's innermost nature filled with hidden, unconscious causes of behavior.

Crabb teaches that behavior is **directly** related to substantive needs in the unconscious.[3] His five propositions on motivation relate to the power of the unconscious on both the conscious mind and on behavior. In his first proposition Crabb says:

> Motivation typically depends upon a need state, or in simpler language, we are motivated to meet our needs.[4]

His "need state" and "needs" refer to security and significance in the unconscious. He presents the same idea in his description of the image of God with its longings for relationship and impact.[5]

Crabb's second proposition refers to unconscious beliefs about how to satisfy the two deep and profound needs. He says:

> Motivation is a word referring to the energy or force which results in specific behavior. . . . I am motivated to meet a need by doing certain things which *I believe in my mind* will meet that need.[6] (Italics his.)

The words *in my mind* refer to the entire Freudian notion of the iceberg. In other words, motivation comes largely from those beliefs in the unconscious having to do with meeting the two needs.

According to Crabb, behavior is not only motivated by unconscious beliefs, but directed by them. In his third proposition, he says:

> Motivated behavior always is directed toward a goal. I believe that *something* will meet my need. That something becomes my goal.[7] (Italics his.)

Conscious choices are therefore goal-oriented and motivated by unconscious beliefs about how to satisfy the two needs. This proposition agrees with Adler's emphasis on all behavior being goal-directed by needs in the unconscious.

In his fourth proposition on motivation, Crabb says:

> When the goal cannot be reached . . . a state of disequilibrium exists (subjectively felt as anxiety). The need which is denied satisfaction becomes a source of negative emotions. . . . I then am motivated to protect my need to feel worthwhile from further injury by minimizing my feelings of insignificance or insecurity.[8]

Crabb emphasizes denial of feelings and self-protection strategies throughout all of his books. In *Inside Out* Crabb refers to "retreat into denial," running from pain through denial, and "a powerless lifestyle of denial."[9]

In his final summary proposition on motivation Crabb declares:

> All behavior is motivated. . . . In order to understand any unit of behavior, **you must know what need is motivating the behavior**. . . .[10] (Bold added.)

This final proposition brings us full circle, back to **motivating needs in the unconscious**, to which, in his closed system, every action is ultimately connected.

Crabb illustrates how his theory of motivation works in a person. This person describes his problem in terms of what he has learned about his wrong assumptions about how to meet his unconscious needs:

> I listen to the preacher tell me that the love of money is the root of all evil. . . . I fully agree with

what the preacher is telling me, but I still feel an inner drive compulsively spurring me on to make money. I try to shake it but I can't. Prayer, repentance, dedication all make me feel better for a while, but the lust for money remains strong. My real problem is not a love of money but rather a wrong belief, a learned assumption that personal significance depends on having money. *Until that idea is deliberately and consciously rejected, I will always want money*, no matter how many times I confess to God my sin of wanting money. . . . But again, as long as **I unconsciously believe that money equals significance, I will never stop lusting after money because I always will be motivated to meet my needs.**[11] (Italics his; bold added.)

The man has obviously learned Crabb's system and terminology. He identifies his problem as "a wrong belief, a learned assumption that personal significance depends on having money," and he thinks that his unconscious belief causes him to lust for money. He has thus concluded that his lust for money is motivated by unconscious needs rather than by the law of sin in his life. But, the heart of his problem is not simply an unconscious assumption about gaining significance; it is sin reigning in his life. He is still self-serving in wanting to be important, to be seen as successful, to be regarded highly, and to control his own life. The Bible does not interpret such self-service in light of psychological needs in the unconscious.

Motivation

There is no debate over the significance of the issue of motivation. Crabb is attempting to address a very vital area of counseling. However, in attempting to wed the issue of motivation to his psychological system of unconscious needs, he has moved away from the doctrine of the Scriptures. In Romans 6-8, Galatians 5 and elsewhere, the Bible speaks of only two "laws" of motivation: the law of sin and the law of the Spirit. The law of sin speaks of a person under the power or rule of sin, and the law of the Spirit speaks of the rulership of the indwelling Holy Spirit. The Bible does not even hint at any third law such as Crabb's proposal of unconscious psychological needs that motivate behavior. Yet Crabb is attempting to make this third law the primary source of information.

The historic position of the Christian church has viewed sin as inherent rebellion, as a corrupt nature, and as the internal tyrant of the heart. Its corrupting power makes the heart deceitful and unknowable apart from God. Unbelievers are under the power of sin. But believers, who have been redeemed and given new life, are enabled to resist the power of sin through the power of the indwelling Holy Spirit. The Bible always assigns the inner motivating powers in light of these two realities. And the Bible never defines indwelling sin as unconscious beliefs related to unconscious needs. It never explains either the role of the Spirit or the power of sin in light of powerful entities in the unconscious known as needs or longings or passions.

The Holy Spirit motivates and enables believers to love and obey God. The apostle John declared, "God is love" (John 4:8). And then he said, "Herein is love, not that we loved God, but that He loved us, and sent us His son to be the propitiation for our sins. Beloved, if God so loved us, we ought also to love one another" (John 4:10-11). Here is the motivation of the person who is walking according to the Spirit rather than according to his old sinful, self-serving ways. The only way a person can follow the Great Commandment to love God with all of his heart, soul, mind and strength is by Jesus' life mediated to the sinner by the Holy Spirit. The Holy Spirit illumines the Word, assures the believer of sonship with the Father, guides the believer, and enables him to love and obey.

> For as many as are led by the Spirit of God, they are the sons of God. For ye have not received the spirit of bondage again to fear; but ye have received the Spirit of adoption, whereby we cry, Abba, Father. The Spirit itself beareth witness with our spirit, that we are the children of God: And if children, then heirs; heirs of God, and joint-heirs with Christ; if so be that we suffer with him, that we may be also glorified together. (Romans 8:14-17.)

The focus of the Bible in relationship to sanctification is not on so-called psychological needs, but on knowing and obeying the will of God (Romans 6:11-13). It is on conscious obedience, on conscious warfare against known temptations and transgressions, and on conscious submission to the power of the Spirit (Galatians 5:16-25 and Romans 8:13). Through God's enabling, it is possible to change attitudes, thoughts, and behavior without fully knowing motives. God does not promise to expose and reveal all of the tangled motives of anyone's heart.

The motivation for Christian living is not inherent within believers in the form of unsatisfied unconscious needs, longings or passions. Rather it lies in the person of Christ (Galatians 2:20). It is outside of people and only becomes a part of them through the gracious intervention of God into their inner man. Christ motivates them to obey God by mediating grace to them in the person of the Holy Spirit. Thus God never speaks of motivation in terms of a simplistic theory of all-powerful unconscious needs.

Psychological Sources

Crabb's language and theory of motivation come right out of psychology.[12] For instance, the following words and ideas of Abraham Maslow closely parallel some of Crabb's words and ideas concerning the relationship of personal needs to motivation.

> All people in our society . . . have a need or desire for a stable, firmly based, usually high evaluation of themselves, for self-respect, or self-esteem, and for the esteem of others. These needs may therefore be classified into two subsidiary sets. These are, first, the desire for strength, for achievement, for adequacy, for mastery and competence, for confidence in the face of the world, and for independence and freedom. Second, we have what we may call the desire for reputation or prestige (defining it as respect or esteem from other people), status, dominance, recognition, attention, importance, or appreciation.[13]

Notice the similarity to Crabb's idea that people need to have a sense of personal worthwhileness, with the subcategories being significance and security. Maslow's writings also teach that needs profoundly affect conscious behavior. He says:

> But thwarting of these needs produces feelings of inferiority, or weakness, and of helplessness.[14]

. . . a healthy man is primarily **motivated by his needs** to develop and actualize his fullest potentialities.[15] (Bold added.)

Does the Bible teach that an unredeemed person will reach his full potential through the satisfaction of all-powerful, hidden needs? Without God's gracious intervention, no one is spiritually healthy. Rather than reaching some great potential of self-actualization, one's own lusts will drive him into sin and rebellion and ultimately to death and hell. But, someone may argue that what Maslow says does apply to Christians because God enables them to develop their full potentialities. Yet, we will only become what God has designed us to become by the motivation that comes from His life in us and from our great love for Him in response to His love for us. How can a new man in Christ continue to be motivated by self or self's needs? It is a contradiction to Jesus' call to deny self, take up one's cross, and follow Him.

The Nature of Man

In defining man's innermost nature, Crabb's distinction between a believer and an unbeliever remains fuzzy. His descriptions of the human seem to apply to all people, believer and unbeliever. Crabb says:

The intangible identity that I know as "Me" has two real and profound needs, which are substantive personal realities not reducible to biological or chemical analysis. They have a personal existence, independent of the physical body, that constitutes the core of what it means to be a spirit.[16]

That is his definition of the biblical term spirit. He then says,

> The image of God is reflected in these two needs. God is a personal being who in His essential nature is *love* and who, as a God of design and purpose, is the author of *meaning*.[17] (Italics his.)

Crabb teaches that since human nature is limited because of the fall, the attributes of man created in the image of God become human needs. For him the corruption of the fall is that capacities for love and meaning (identical of the needs for security and significance in Crabb's system) are filled in the wrong ways.

While it is true that fallen man does try to fulfill his needs and desires in wrong ways, the essence of the fall is more than simply how a person fulfills his needs. At the Fall, love and meaning became self-centered and self-directed. Love for God was replaced with love for self. God's purposes and will were replaced by self-will. Love was distorted and misdirected and self became its own little god. The essence of natural man is sin, not unmet needs for security and significance.

But Crabb's view of the human heart makes no distinction before or after conversion in the essence of its so-called legitimate longings. In *Understanding People* Crabb says:

> The longings of the human heart, I submit, cannot be changed. And even if they could, to do so would make mankind less than God designed us to be. Our longings are legitimate. . . . The problem is not centrally with our longings.[18]

And yet, the entire New Testament argues that the long-ings do change. The desire to please self is replaced by a desire to love and please God.

Jesus made a clear distinction between the nature of a believer saved by grace through faith and the nature of an unredeemed sinner. (John 15.) He made a distinction between the children of God and the children of the devil. (John 8:44 and 10:27-29.) Paul made these same distinc-tions throughout his letter to the Ephesians. John said that the world does not even know (understand) the sons of God. (John 3:1.)

Some of the unredeemed may very well identify with much of what psychology says, because self (with all of its self-seeking, self-regard, self-will, self-excusing, self-blaming, self-love, self-worth, self-fulfillment, and self-pity) is at the center. And Christians can become confused when they see that they, who have been liberated from the domination of sin, still struggle against its power (Romans 6-8). However, they are nevertheless new cre-ations in Christ. John describes it this way:

> But as many as received him, to them gave he power to become the sons of God, even to them that believe on his name: Which were born, not of blood, nor of the will of the flesh, nor of the will of man, but of God. (John 1:12-13.)

The believer has God's life in him. And it is the very Spirit of God who enables him to love God and others.

Crabb's Thirst

Crabb reiterates his psychological theory of uncon-scious need motivation in biblical garb. He uses the metaphors in John 7:37-38 to present his psychological understanding of the capacities of personhood:

> If any man thirst, let him come unto me, and drink. He that believeth on me, as the scripture hath said, out of his belly shall flow rivers of living water.

From these few words Crabb develops an elaborate system of Thirsty Souls to verify his theory of motivational needs/ longings and Hollow Cores to verify his theory of the unconscious. Crabb says that Jesus came to quench thirst, but that the Scriptures "seem quiet on the subject." In fact he declares, "Thirst is never defined."[19] Crabb tells us that even the apostle Paul failed to clear up the meaning of this crucial theme. He contends that until now the real issue of thirst has been largely neglected.[20] It seems a little odd to call something a biblical theme and then to say that Scriptures are strangely silent on the exact meaning of the theme.

However, the word *thirst* as used in the Bible has not been neglected. In the above passage, *thirst* is a metaphor referring to intense spiritual desire for knowing God and experiencing His presence. In the above instance, the context tells us that the thirst Jesus quenches leads to an abundant, overflowing life resulting from the indwelling Holy Spirit. It is thus a thirst for God, His presence, His revelation, and His righteousness. Jesus said, "Blessed are they that do hunger and thirst after righteousness, for they shall be filled" (Matthew 5:6). Words carry their own meanings, but when used as metaphors, their meaning is revealed through the context in which they are used. Thus the meaning of *thirst* has not been a mystery through the ages. One can turn to lexicons, Bible dictionaries, commentaries, sermons, and devotional literature and come across the word *thirst* in the context of where and how it is used in the Bible.

Since Crabb erroneously contends that thirst is "never defined," he says:

> If we permit ourselves to ask only those questions that the Bible *explicitly* answers, we must put aside our questions about thirst and move on to other matters.[21] (Italics his.)

Crabb then gives his own **psychological definition** of *thirst*: deep longing for relationship and impact. The words *thirst* and *longings* function as technical terms for Crabb. They refer to much more than the average person would imply when using them. Crabb defines personhood in terms of unrelenting thirst for the satisfaction of the two needs/longings that are vital, powerful, profound realities of the Hollow Core. They cannot be ignored; they cry out for satisfaction. He says, "As image-bearers designed to enjoy God and everything He has made, we are thirsty people who long for what was lost in the Fall."[22] At first this may sound orthodox, but from the evidence throughout his books, what he contends was lost is the satisfaction of the needs for security and significance, also referred to as relationship and impact.[23]

The word *thirsty* in the context of Crabb's books signifies the unrelenting drive for satisfaction of the "*deep longings in the human heart for relationship and impact,*" which are really the "*personal needs for security and significance.*"[24] Therefore he is talking about a Freudian-like unconscious with needs that motivate behavior. Thus, any longing for relationship with God in this context is to meet the needs of the self. Remember that the central need behind the needs for security and significance is the need for regarding oneself as worthwhile.[25]

Besides John 7:36-37, Crabb cites Psalms 42:2 and 63:1, Isaiah 55:1, and John 6:35 in defense of his theory of unconscious needs/longings. Each passage uses the word *thirst*. However, to cite passages which speak of "longing (thirsting) for God" as support for his doctrine of Need Theology is invalid. The Psalms describe the **believer** as longing for God, not for the satisfaction of two unconscious needs that constantly press for gratification. None of the passages teach Crabb's concept of two substantive, all-powerful needs/longings at the core of man's being.

Because Crabb comes to the Bible with his theory of two needs/longings firmly fixed in his model of man, he sees hidden implications in biblical passages. Thus it appears that he does not seek answers to man's innermost nature from the clearly intended meaning of the biblical text. Rather, he seeks confirmation. A determination to understand the Bible's clearly intended meaning should prevent one from being satisfied with hidden implications for documentation.

The Personal Circle as a Hollow Core

Crabb amplifies his theme of thirst with what he calls a "Hollow Core." And he uses the same verse for a biblical reference:

> If any man thirst, let him come unto me, and drink. He that believeth on me, as the scripture hath said, out of his belly shall flow rivers of living water (John 7:37-38).

Crabb does not explain the purpose and content of the Lord's invitation. Nor does he explain its relationship to regeneration and the workings of the Holy Spirit. Crabb's interest centers on the Greek term *koilia*, which is translated "innermost being." Here is his line of reasoning: (1) *Koilia* refers to a deep part within the core of our being. (2) *Koilia* literally means an open, empty space. Metaphorically it refers to an empty space that "desperately longs to be filled."[26] (3) Therefore, everyone has a Hollow Core that is empty, but yearns to be filled. The awful emptiness is caused by everyone's two unfilled needs/ longings. Crabb leaps from the mere definition of *koilia* to an elaborate theory of a so-called Hollow Core with its identifiable content and incredible powers. Not only has one word become an entire theory; it becomes the drama of an empty core with "monstrous power" which controls the direction of every person's life.[27]

On the basis of **implication**, which he draws from the word *koilia*, Crabb presents a "dimension of personality" that he calls the "Hollow Core." Then he takes a principle from the natural world and uses it to explain the dynamics of that Hollow Core by saying:

> Nature, whether physical or personal, abhors a vacuum. Internal emptiness becomes an absolutely compelling force that drives people to sacrifice anything, eventually even their own identities, in an effort to find themselves.[28]

Crabb jumps from the biblical term *koilia* into a strictly defined theory about an internal vacuum that controls the very direction of a person's life. He takes a quantum leap from a single verse to a definitive doctrine about an "absolutely compelling force" driving people's lives from deep within their being. Here are some of the things he says about the Hollow Core:

But when the Hollow Core is empty . . . our **souls
are torn apart** with an **unbearable ache**, a throbbing loneliness that **demands relief**, a morbid
sense of pointlessness that **paralyzes** us with
anger, cynicism, and frustration.[29] (Bold added.)

. . . it becomes a **monstrous power** that **relent-
lessly controls** the core direction of our lives.[30]
(Bold added.)

. . . if the **horrible reality of the Hollow Core**
remains unchanged, the counselee remains a **slave**
to the god of his own longings for satisfaction.[31]
(Bold added.)

An unsaved sinner will indeed remain a "slave to the
god of his own longings for satisfaction" unless he is
saved. But for Crabb the Hollow Core is the unconscious,
not the old nature dominated by sin.

The all-powerful motivational factors in the unconscious continue to be Crabb's dominant explanation of
behavior. For example, in describing one woman, he says:

Doubt and lust became **overpowering obsessions**
she could not escape. **Beneath** it all was a **terribly
frustrated longing** to have someone see all of her
and remain deeply involved.[32] (Bold added.)

Crabb graphically describes the thirst in the Hollow Core
when he says: "The pain of aloneness and pointlessness is
piercing. It *demands* relief."[33] (Italics his.)

Along with his expanded use of the word *koilia*, Crabb
says that in John 7:37-38, "the Lord appeals directly to
this deep ache" in our Hollow Core.[34] Thus, he must
believe that the Lord had the same concept in mind and

spoke directly to this aching, empty, pain-filled Hollow
Core. Yet, consider the implications. First, recall briefly
that Crabb identifies the content and power of the Hollow
Core as the deep needs/longings. The hollowness or
emptiness of the Core is caused directly by failure to satisfy those deep needs/longings.[35] If they are unsatisfied
they produce an unbearable ache, throbbing loneliness,
paralyzing anger, cynicism, and frustration.[36] Crabb
describes the Hollow Core with its content and power in
much the same way as he describes the unconscious.[37]
Therefore, Crabb is attempting to make the Lord's invitation function as a defense for his psychological theories of
the unconscious, of powerful unconscious needs/ longings,
and of the unconscious strategies to satisfy the two
needs/longings.

In his argument for the Hollow Core, Crabb demon-
strates how his psychological preoccupation controls his
biblical interpretation. But, he has not demonstrated that
Jesus used the term *koilia* to refer to the two needs in the
unconscious and the unconscious strategies for satisfying
them. If Jesus had taught about a Hollow Core producing
pain and driving people in disastrous directions, he would
have been talking about the old sinful self, fulfilling its
lustful desires. But for Crabb, the Hollow Core is the residence of the two legitimate needs/longings.

9

Limits of Consciousness

According to Crabb's model of man, the unconscious plays a powerful role. Besides the unconscious being filled with powerful, motivating needs and longings, problems occur because the unconscious also contains many faulty and damaging messages and beliefs that control and direct conscious activity.[1] While Freud developed the original theory of the unconscious, it was Adler who called the faulty beliefs and messages "guiding fictions." In the course of his writings, Crabb uses such phrases as "basic assumptions,"[2] "wrong strategies,"[3] and "relational strategies."[4] All of his labels refer to the same thing, namely, a person's wrong, damaging beliefs, assumptions, or strategies about how to satisfy the deepest needs/longings/passions. They are always relegated to

163

the unconscious (beneath the surface, inside, etc.) and they are in the Rational Circle of Crabb's Four-Circle model.

Beliefs and Strategies

Crabb's teaching on false assumptions and wrong strategies may be summarized briefly. Painful disappointments are created by the failure to satisfy the unconscious needs/longings/passions. The drive to satisfy them is so earnest and consuming that people develop strategies for satisfying them from early childhood on. The strategies then move into the unconscious, the original location of the unconscious needs. The strategies are wrong in that they cannot provide the lasting satisfaction that the person seeks to gain.

Even though the strategies cannot succeed, people still operate according to the dictates of those unconscious wrong assumptions. Since firmly-held beliefs in the unconscious direct an individual's conduct, a person's main problem is his unconsciously-held false assumptions. Hence Crabb, along with Adler, teaches that in order to truly understand and help people, one must unearth and change their unconscious programs.[5] For example, in the midst of his discussion on the unconscious, he says,

> There are, I believe, processes going on within our personalities that determine the directions we move, the strategies we use to protect ourselves from personal circle pain and to pursue anticipated pleasure.[6]

"Personal circle pain" refers to the failure to satisfy the two deepest needs/longings. The "strategies" refer to the unconsciously-held assumptions about how to satisfy the two needs.

Crabb's ideas about his Rational Circle have been influenced by Albert Ellis's Rational Emotive Behavior Therapy, which is a system of changing thoughts and beliefs in order to change behavior. Ellis's own humanistic belief system focuses on self-acceptance, self-affirmation, self-effort, and self-talk to reprogram the mind. Crabb says:

> My thesis is that problems develop when the basic needs for significance and security are threatened. People pursue irresponsible ways of living as a means of defending against feelings of insignificance and insecurity. In most cases these folks have arrived at a wrong idea as to what constitutes significance and security. And these **false beliefs are at the core of their problems**.[7] (Bold added.)

Crabb then quotes Proverbs 23:7 as supposed biblical support: "As [a man] thinketh in his heart, so is he." However, the context of the verse does not support his statement. This is just one example of how Crabb misuses Scripture in his attempt to give biblical support to his psychology. Proverbs 23:7 is actually a warning to watch out for duplicity:

> Eat thou not the bread of him that hath an evil eye, neither desire thou his dainty meats: For as he thinketh in his heart, so is he: Eat and drink, saith he to thee; but his heart is not with thee. The morsel which thou has eaten shalt thou vomit up, and lose thy sweet words. (Proverbs 23:6-8.)

The "he" referred to in Proverbs 23:7 is a person not to be trusted. The passage cannot be used to teach that if a person changes his unconscious beliefs he will overcome problems related to feelings of insecurity and insignificance.

The following quotations demonstrate that Crabb consistently promotes this concept of unconscious wrong beliefs and strategies. In his 1975 book, *Basic Principles of Biblical Counseling*, Crabb says:

> The two critical points to understand are, first, that each of us tends to unconsciously perceive the world of people (at least the world of people close to us) in a rather stereotyped fashion which was learned in childhood, and, second, we entertain a basic belief about what pattern of behavior is appropriate in our world to meet our personal needs. To the degree that that belief is in error we will experience problems in living.[8]

Later in *Effective Biblical Counseling* (1977) Crabb describes the unconscious as *"the reservoir of basic assumptions which people firmly and emotionally hold about how to meet their needs of significance and security."*[9] (Italics his.) He then declares that each person has been "programmed in his or her unconscious mind."[10] He continues:

> We all develop some *wrong assumptions* about how to get our needs met. . . . We often are not aware of our basic wrong belief about how to meet our needs. Yet that ungodly belief determines how we evaluate the things happening to us in our world and that evaluation in turn controls our feeling and behavior.[11] (Italics his.)

Then in *Marriage Builder* (1982), he says:

> Imbedded in our make-up are certain beliefs about how to become worthwhile or how to avoid injury to our self-esteem, how to be happy or how to avoid pain. . . each of us reliably develops wrong beliefs about how to find the meaning and love we need. And a belief about what I need implies a goal that I should pursue. . . . *Beliefs determine goals.*[12] (Italics his.)

In this context, beliefs are unconscious even though the goals may be conscious. In the same book he gives several examples, including this one:

> Suppose a boy is reared by parents who neglect him to pursue their own interests. He may develop the belief that there is no one who will attend to his needs. That wrong belief may lead him to strive for *absolute self-reliance* as the goal he must achieve to avoid personal pain.[13] (Italics his.)

Crabb's 1987 book, *Understanding People*, continues the same theme. In his section "Contents of the Unconscious," he says:

> But still the pain exists, and we are motivated to find relief. As relational beings we devise strategies for responding to life that will keep the pain out of awareness and, we hope, gain at least a measure of the satisfaction we want. The particular strategies we develop emerge as the product of our images of ourselves and the world and our beliefs about what can be done.[14]

According to Crabb's diagram in the same section, the beliefs, images, and pain are all in the unconscious.[15] He describes the unconscious strategies further:

> . . . beneath every method of relating can be found a commitment to self-interest, a determination to protect oneself from more relational pain . . . the sinfully wrong strategies by which we manipulate people with our well-being in mind are intentionally hidden from view. They take their place in the unconscious.[16]

In his 1988 book, *Inside Out*, Crabb says:

> An inside look, then, can be expected to uncover two elements imbedded deeply in our heart: (1) thirst or *deep longings* for what we do not have; and (2) stubborn independence reflected in *wrong strategies* for finding the life we desire.[17] (Italics his.)

In the same book Crabb relegates the two longings and wrong strategies to the unconscious.[18] According to Crabb, personal problems can be traced to unconscious wrong assumptions.[19] In *Connecting* (1997), Crabb continues to speak of "Denied Longings," "Self-Preserving Dynamics," and a "Basic Life Strategy."[20]

Deep Fear, Self-Protection, and Thick Layers

Another foundational concept in Crabb's model is a view of self-protection based upon Freudian ego-defense mechanisms. Self-deception is part of the entire schema of the unconscious, with its needs, power, strategies, and motives. In his book *Encouragement: The Key to Caring*,

Crabb paints the scenario of a businessman named Vic.[21] Vic outwardly shows signs of success. He is also pleasant, personable, and socially at ease in most public situations. However, no one, including Vic, truly knows the "real Vic." Why this ignorance of the "real Vic"? Crabb begins to tell us by saying, "Beneath the look of confidence lies deep fear: 'I have to be more successful than dad or I'll be unhappy just like him.'" After describing Vic's external success, Crabb continues:

> Because Vic is a professing Christian, part of his success package includes church attendance, prayer before mealtimes, and occasional family devotions. **But all these things serve to hide, even from himself, the deep sense of inadequacy that drives him toward the visible reminders of success. His fear is deep, his layers thick.**[22] (Bold added.)

According to Crabb, "no one *really* knows him." (Italics his.) Not only that, Vic doesn't even know how miserable he really is. Crabb says:

> His fears remain conveniently shielded from view, so well hidden that not even he is aware that his purpose in living is to prove a point and reduce a fear. . . . Because fear continues to quietly dominate his life, his layers stay firmly in place, thickened to the point that he will let nothing puncture his false sense of security. Vic is blind to his own spiritual poverty.[23]

Crabb contends that no one knows the "real Vic" because even though everything may be just fine on the conscious level, a man may well be seething with terror and undermined by inadequacy at the unconscious level.

Thus Crabb analyzes Vic as having deep unconscious "fear," hidden by thick "layers" built up to protect a fragile self-image. Therefore, to get at the real Vic one must "peel away" those "self-protective layers" and expose the unconscious world of pain, fear, and emptiness. This Freudian notion that a man may be consciously happy while unconsciously miserable, consciously peaceful while unconsciously terrorized, and consciously confident while unconsciously fearful permeates Crabb's books.[24] It is a duality that has no support in the Bible.

All of the confidence about what is inside makes it seem that psychologists have inside knowledge, that they can read right past the layers into the unconscious. What a psychologist says may indeed sound plausible to someone who has placed confidence in him. However, if a counselee does not agree that he is miserable and frustrated on the inside while he is happy and peaceful on the outside, he may very well be accused of denial and self-protection. Carol Tavris, in her book *Anger: The Misunderstood Emotion* describes what can happen with this kind of Freudian mind-set. She says:

> Sitting in a cafe one afternoon, I overheard the following exchange between two women:
> Woman A: "You'll feel better if you get your anger out."
> Woman B: "Anger? Why am I angry?"
> Woman A: "Because he left you, that's why."
> Woman B: "Left me? What are you talking about? He *died*. He was an *old man*."
> Woman A: "Yes, but to your unconscious it's no different from abandonment. Underneath, you are

blaming him for not keeping his obligation to you to protect you forever."

Woman B: "That might have been true if I were ten years old, Margaret, but I'm forty-two, we both knew he was dying, and we had time to make our peace. I don't feel angry, I feel sad. I *miss* him. He was a darling father to me."

Woman A: "Why are you so defensive? Why are you denying your true feelings? Why are you afraid of therapy?"

Woman B: "Margaret, *you are driving me crazy. I don't feel angry, dammit!*"

Woman A (*smiling*): "So why are you shouting?"

It is not entirely easy to argue with a Freudian devotee, because disagreement is usually taken as denial or "blocking."[25] (Italics hers.)

Crabb would no doubt call that an amateur attempt at getting past the layers, but he does emphasize the same theme of defensive self-protection through the denial of real feelings.

The technique of denial is well-known to Freudians as one of the ego defense mechanisms. People supposedly build defensive layers to avoid the excruciating pain of facing the emptiness and disappointments existing in their unconscious. According to the theory, they are terrified at the thought of honestly facing their unconscious pain. Hence, people are primarily motivated by fear. They are unconsciously terrified!

Crabb teaches that the central motivational power known as fear drives all men to build self-protective layers. He says that "fear consumes the core of every person."[26] In his model, fear is the core motivation behind everything. Crabb explains its relationship to our two needs:

Because we are fallen beings, our capacities have
become desperate longings energized by a fear that
we will never find the satisfaction we desire.[27]

Thus, according to Crabb, everyone is thus energized
by fear at the unconscious core of his being. At the core,
all are driven by fear to protect self from the pain of
unmet needs. That is an amazing description of all people! What about Paul and the apostles? Were they driven
by fear to evangelize the world? What about missionaries
who have given their lives for the sake of the gospel? And
although some people are driven by fear because they are
not trusting and obeying God, one cannot define all motivation with the single word *fear*.

Crabb contends that fear and denial constitute a
fundamental problem with most Christians. He especially
criticizes seminary graduates, pastors, and professors as
poorly equipped to handle the problems of real people in
the real world because they are unaware of the real difficulties of life.[28] He suggests that these men are ill-
equipped because they too are caught in the jaws of
pretense, denial, and self-protection. But, of course, they
are not aware of this because it is unconscious.[29]

Crabb emphasizes denial of feelings and self-protective strategies throughout his books. In *Inside Out* Crabb
refers to "retreat into denial," running from pain through
denial, and "a powerless lifestyle of denial."[30] He says,
"Perhaps much of what passes for spiritual maturity is
maintained by a rigid denial of all that is happening
beneath the surface of their lives."[31] Crabb says that
self-protecting strategies build "insulating layers of
friendliness and appropriate involvement [which] work to
keep us from touching the terrible pain of previously felt
disappointment."[32] Thus even the finest qualities and
godly activities can be condemned by Crabb as being

sinful, because they may appear to prevent one from centering on the pain of disappointment.

According to Crabb, Christians must honestly face the painful material in their unconscious if they want to grow. But, in order to gain an honest look at the inside, they must discover and then discard their self-protective strategies.[33] He contends that refusal to "honestly face" all of that pain stored in the unconscious is the chief cause of shallow Christian living. In Crabb's opinion, such denial leads to shallow conformity, judgmentalism, and legalism.[34]

Again, Crabb lays some of the blame for that shallowness on the evangelical seminaries, because they have failed to prepare ministers to psychologically deal with pain, beliefs, and images in the unconscious mind.[35] Hence, ministers deal only with the conscious mind and leave the crucial contents of the unconscious unattended. The implication is that this lack is the reason why so many churches are in such a low state of spiritual vigor. Concerned about shepherds who only deal with the tip of the iceberg, while neglecting the great mass of unconscious pain, beliefs, and images,[36] Crabb says:

> We rarely consider the value of what I believe is central to real change: taking a hard look at the commitment to self-protection that displays itself most clearly in our ways of relating to people.[37]

He then illustrates his point:

> The gentle pastor has convinced others *and himself* that his patience is the fruit of the Spirit, when it may be nothing more than ugly self-protection. To change from the inside out requires that we repent of our self-protective commitment.[38] (Italics his.)

According to Crabb, the gentle pastor is not aware of unconscious pain, fear, and strategies which explain the motives of his behavior. Hence, he has deceived himself and others through his self-protective "style of relating."[39]

Crabb's counseling involves stripping away those self-protective layers to get to the real person hiding underneath. Moreover, in Crabb's integration model, the very essence of Christian sanctification involves deep probing into the unconscious.

Does the Bible Support Crabb's Theory of Self-Protection?

Crabb discusses the concept of self-protection at length and regularly imposes it upon various biblical passages. However, he does not demonstrate that either the intent or the context of any Bible passage agrees with his psychological notion of self-protection. An example of his psychological view of Scripture can be seen in his interpretation of the doctrine of repentance in light of his notion on self-protection.[40] He contends that repentance must involve insight into one's own inner pain that "triggered" the outward sin. One must recognize that beneath the sinful behavior there is the greater sin for which he must repent: the sin of self-protection.

According to Crabb, one cannot truly repent without the process of insight into so-called unconscious needs that cry out for fulfillment. Without biblical support, Crabb contends that a Christian has only half-repented if he does not take self-protection into account. He gives an example of a man who loses his temper and yells at his wife. If he only confesses his sinful behavior, his repentance is not complete. He must become aware of his "relational pain and protective strategies" if he is to repent more fully.[41]

Moreover, Crabb contends that a person must realize that he himself has been a victim before he can even understand his sinful commitment to self-protection and then repent at his deepest level. Crabb says:

> I believe there's a simple reason why sin in the heart, that commitment to self-protection that manifests itself in so many defensive styles of relating, is so rarely recognized as deep and serious. We can't recognize self-protection until we see what we're protecting. Until we face our disappointment as a victim, we cannot clearly identify the strategies we've adopted to insulate ourself from further disappointment. *Only a deep awareness of our own profound disappointment (pain in our heart) can enable us to realize our desires for satisfaction have become demands for relief (sin in our heart).*[42] (Italics his.)

He declares that it is necessary to get "in touch with the damage to our soul **caused by other people's sinfulness**" in order to identify and repent of the "sin in the heart, that commitment to self-protection."[43] (Bold added.) Thus he reverses the way of repentance, asking people first to focus on the sins of **others**. Talking about and reexperiencing the sins committed against one are Crabb's proposed activities for initiating real repentance. But, the Bible does not teach believers to focus on, talk about, and reexperience the pain of past sins committed against them. These activities are not biblical requirements preceding forgiveness of others.

Crabb offers no Scripture that verifies his theory of repentance. Nor are there any Scriptures that warrant subsuming the doctrine of repentance under psychological ideas of self-protection and rehearsing the sins of others. Rather than laying a proper biblical foundation, Crabb presents lengthy discussions that wed psychological theories of ego-defense mechanisms to the biblical doctrine of repentance and forgiveness.

The Limits of Consciousness and Volition

Crabb defines the conscious mind "as that part of the person which makes conscious evaluations including moral judgments."[44] However, Crabb immediately qualifies that definition by saying that the unconscious determines the sentences which people consciously speak to themselves.[45] A person may indeed think consciously and evaluatively. However, according to Crabb, underneath the conscious thinking is a whole host of submerged, but powerful beliefs and images.

Crabb's Volitional and Emotional Circles have both conscious and unconscious material. According to Crabb's system, the conscious mind expresses the content of the unconscious. He teaches that conscious thinking, choosing, acting, and feeling are external responses to contents of the unconscious, especially the pain caused by others not having met a person's needs. Volitional and Emotional Circles only make sense if they are interpreted in light of the Personal and Rational Circles.

Crabb's Volitional Circle is where people make active choices.[46] It represents their capacity to set a direction, choose behavior, and pursue their goal.[47] As noted earlier, Crabb has been influenced by Adler in his emphasis on goal-oriented behavior. Adler gave great importance to his fundamental proposition that "every psychic phenomenon, if it is to give us any understanding of a person, can only be grasped and understood if regarded as a preparation for some goal."[48]

It cannot be disputed that people do make conscious choices about their activities and do set goals. However, what is questionable is the dependence and subservience of Crabb's choices and goals to unconscious needs and strategies. In his model, choices are made on the basis of what lies beneath the waterline, that is, in the unconscious. He gives this example of what might be going on in a person:

> With the **pain of unmet longings driving her** to find relief, and with her images and beliefs guiding her search, the stage is set for a visible direction to emerge as she looks for a way to handle her world. The first element of that direction is a goal. Beliefs about what brings satisfaction always carry with them a goal to be pursued. When someone reaches an understanding of what must be done to relieve personal circle pain, that understanding quickly translates into a goal.[49] (Bold added.)

Unmet needs/longings in the unconscious drive her, and the images and beliefs of the unconscious guide her. And since unmet needs and longings drive her to wrong conclusions and self protective actions, her sin is not her fault, but rather the fault of others who have not met her needs. She is further exonerated by saying that this is beyond her conscious awareness and conscious control, since everything done at the conscious volitional level is under the direction of the unconscious. What kind of choice or responsibility is that?

Emotions

Crabb's Emotional Circle represents the capacity to experience life "with feeling."[50] Again no one will deny that emotions are a very real part of human existence. However in Crabb's system, the emotions, like the will, are predicated upon what lurks beneath the waterline. According to Crabb's perspective, emotions can be understood only as they are interpreted in light of the unconscious content of the Personal and Rational Circles. In fact, according to Crabb, the emotions of many people may be largely submerged in the unconscious so that they do not consciously feel their deep emotions. Thus, the only way to grasp the significance of human emotions is to view them through the narrow perspective of Crabb's unproven theory of the unconscious.

Conscious and unconscious emotions play a large part in the kind of psychological counseling that is based upon theories of the unconscious and hierarchy of needs. Here emotions can serve to make a person vulnerable to change. They can be like cracks in the layers of self-protective strategies. According to this theory, if an event occurs to touch the emotions, a person becomes vulnerable and may either become defensive and add to his layers of self-protection or be willing to experience the emotion. Thus an emotional experience can serve as a wedge through the supposed layers of self-protection to expose contents of the unconscious. Furthermore, when insight occurs an emotional response is expected.

The emotions that Crabb elicits are those of disappointment and pain that the counselee feels because of the sins of others. He encourages people to enter their pain and experience their disappointment. He believes that by doing this a person will be driven to God to find satisfaction for thirst. However, such activity may inappropriately serve to relieve a person from guilt feelings. Although Crabb may not see this, the natural consequence of focusing on personal disappointments is relief from guilt. After all, if a person's sin is due to unfulfilled needs, then it's really not his fault that he is sinful. It's really the fault of others and perhaps even God for not fulfilling the needs in more obvious ways.

Appeals for Change

Being willing to change and to go through the painful process of change must occur at the conscious level, even according to Crabb's system. People are responsible for their choices. But how? Rather than making obvious changes at the conscious level, people must choose to really change by being willing to look inside. Yet is that action unconsciously motivated? Perhaps one could say that in Crabb's system the second-worst sin of all is to refuse to look inside to discover the primary sin of self-protection.

Presumably, unless Crabb believes that people can indeed decide to do something about exposing their unconscious material, he would not have bothered to write his books. He uses reason to speak to a person's conscious evaluative thinking in the conscious part of the Rational Circle. Here he seeks to convince people to believe that they can truly change from the inside out, **if** they use his method. He appeals to the Volitional Circle by persuading them to be willing to expose their inner needs and manipulative strategies. And through his real life stories and promises of change and growth, he appeals to the Emotional Circle. He thus addresses the conscious mind to bring people to a point of exposing the so-called unconscious. And through all of the argumentation there is both direct and implicit criticism of those who refuse or resist this kind of processing.

10

The Exposing Process

Crabb's methodology of change primarily involves exposure of what he believes lurks beneath the surface. According to Crabb, any attempt to change without cleaning out the hidden basement (the unconscious) will result in merely superficial external conformity.[1] Counselors thus work to expose what they believe to be self-protective layers which people have supposedly built up in order to avoid the pain stored in the unconscious mind. They try to expose self-protective techniques such as denial as well as the unconscious material itself. The reason they must work on self-protective strategies is because, for Crabb, these constitute the essence of sin. For him sin is primarily all that a person does to prevent or relieve himself of pain brought on by others.

Crabb says that the exposure process is not easy. In fact it is quite difficult and very painful, so much so that the word *pain* is repeated throughout *Inside Out*. It's in the first sentence and on the last page. One learns that, although it's not okay to deny and relate to people from defensive layers, it is okay to hurt. It's not only okay to hurt; it's absolutely essential. Crabb contends that pain is necessary for growth and that most people try to avoid it. Therefore people use all kinds of self-protective measures "to prevent painful unconscious material from becoming conscious."[2] Or, as he says in *Inside Out*, "Most of us cope with life by pretending."[3] Hence, everyone is supposedly involved in denial. There is repeated reference to the Freudian ego-defense mechanisms of denial and repression in the unconscious and self-protective layers, which have been built up to prevent an honest exposure.[4]

According to Crabb, deep change requires work from the inside (unconscious) to the outside. It consists of stripping away the self-protective layers. Crabb says:

> Many of the people we deal with in counseling are hiding behind all sorts of defensive overlays designed to protect a fragile sense of self-acceptance or to prevent further rejection or failure from reaching an already crippled self-identity. Counseling involves a **stripping away of the layers, sometimes gently, sometimes forcefully**, to reach the real person underneath. The context of all such efforts must be genuine acceptance, or as Rogers puts it, unconditional positive regard for the worth of the individual.[5] (Bold added.)

The exposing process can be gentle but firm nudging, through encouraging the person to talk about his feelings. Crabb suggests a way to do this:

Start by asking for feedback about yourself: "I think I have a hard time getting really close to people. I've wondered if I communicate that I'm too busy or too important for real friendship. I'd appreciate hearing how each of you experiences me in this group, even right now as I share this. **How do I make you feel?**"[6] (Bold added.)

As a person focuses on his feelings, he supposedly gains insight into his unconscious.

Not only will a therapist encourage the admission and expression of feelings, he may sometimes seek to evoke those emotions. However, Crabb cautions that not just anybody should try this. He says that *"meaningful involvement must precede efforts to expose each other's sin."* (Italics his.) He continues:

No one should appoint himself Minister of Exposure to the entire congregation. When someone tells me I come across as pushy, my ability to receive that input well depends partly on how persuaded I am that the one who's given the input genuinely cares about me.[7]

Thus, exposure can be quite direct. But, according to Crabb, as long as all is done with Rogers' "unconditional positive regard" and the right motive, almost anything can be said to expose what might be lurking beneath the surface.[8] Direct or implied accusations of denial may also be used to expose a person's self-protective strategies.

Crabb also recommends group involvement in exposing layers and strategies as well as individual counseling. And while harm is not intended, such a process can result in personal attack in order to puncture holes in the layers so that the person can finally see **that** he is denying and **what** he is denying.

In *The Journal of Humanistic Psychology*, John Rowan describes what happens in the secular setting:

> I have seen people bullied and intimidated in groups because they weren't expressing feelings, or even because they weren't expressing the *right* feelings, such as anger. . . . I have even seen people criticized because they weren't expressing feelings *all the time*![9] (Italics his.)

Notice the importance of feelings. In the kind of therapy that seeks to unearth hidden motives and beliefs in the unconscious, an emotional response is expected to accompany insight. If there is not enough strong emotion, it may indicate that the layers have not been penetrated. Thus a strong emotion is like a sign that progress is being made.

Although Crabb would no doubt deny ever intimidating or bullying anyone, the very process of exposure itself can be quite intimidating. Also, a subtle verbal and non-verbal bullying and intimidation can occur in the process of attempting to expose the so-called contents of the unconscious. And Crabb does insist that real change requires an exposure of unconscious motives and beliefs.[10] He also emphasizes feelings and believes that strong emotions accompany real insight and growth. In discussing a particular case, he says:

> The first act of changing his current relational style had to be to open himself to **feeling the pain of his past**. Only then would he be in a position to realize how deeply determined he was to never feel that pain again. . . moving on to deeper levels of involve-

ment with others required this man to **more deeply feel his pain** and to face his self-protective sin. The more deeply we enter our disappointment, the more thoroughly we can face our sin. Unless we **feel the pain of being victimized**, we will tend to limit the definition of our problem with sin to visible acts of transgression.[11] (Bold added.)

Notice the emphasis on having been victimized. Rather than facing our own depravity and our own failure to love God and others, we are to concentrate on past offenses that others have committed against us. Practically speaking, the process of talking about the past and acutely feeling disappointments of the past could very well involve dishonoring parents. One wonders where the Bible encourages people to expose the sins of others publicly for one's own benefit. It is certainly the opposite of biblical forgiveness and the admonitions to do good to enemies and overcome evil with good. Furthermore by magnifying disappointments from the past a person could even be encouraged to blame God.

This return to feel the pain of the past is based on the Freudian theory of abreaction. The *Dictionary of Psychology* defines *abreaction* as "the discharge of tension by reliving in words, feelings, and actions" a painful event from the past.[12] Supposedly reliving the pain of past experience relieves a person from its unconscious grip. However, research has never proven this idea. On the other hand, there is great suspicion that quite the reverse is true. Rather than being rid of pain in the unconscious, a person may actually be creating new pain. Although there may be a false relief from guilt and there may be a sense of relief after feeling pain and crying, nothing really changes except a shift in responsibility for the sin and a stronger commitment to the technique of abreaction and the system that incorporates it. Similar forms of abreaction and ensuing commitment occur in rebirthing, primal therapy, inner healing, est, and Gestalt as well as in psychoanalysis.

However, in such settings any really helpful change is not dependent upon those theories or techniques. According to the research, actual change occurs because a person wants to change, not because of the counseling methodology.[13] Therefore, if anyone changes for the better under such a process, it has more to do with personal commitment to change than the process itself. Additionally, a person's expectation for change also has more to do with whether a person changes than with the process or method used. Researcher David Shapiro says that "treatments differ in effectiveness only to the extent that they arouse in clients differing degrees of expectation of benefit."[14]

A method of counseling is always dependent upon the theory behind it. And if one believes that one needs to strip off layers and feel the pain that resides in the unconscious, then "no pain, no gain," or "pain is gain." Not only that, the insight a person gains generally has more to do with what the therapist is looking for than with what is really there. If the therapist looks for a painful past, the counselee will give it to him. If he looks for archetypes in dreams, the counselee will dredge those up. As with all psychotherapeutic systems, everything a person does can be interpreted according to the system.

Crabb not only advocates such exposure in counseling. He encourages small groups to meet together for the same purpose. Rather than Bible study, the members interact to *give feedback lovingly* and to *receive feedback non-defensively*."[15] He gives an example of a small group encouraging a man to focus on his times of disappointment and "his refusal to enter deeply into the experience

of his disappointment."[16] The man's response to the probing was to say, "Am I to focus on my pain and think about
nothing other than how badly I've been victimized? I'm
more interested in knowing how I can get on with my life.
What's past is past. I want to learn to relate effectively to
people now."[17] Crabb then criticizes the man for his "self-
protective commitment to never experience the level of
pain he'd felt in his childhood."[18]

Crabb misuses Scripture to support this practice of
probing.[19] He quotes Hebrews 3:13:

> Take heed, brethren, lest there be in any of you an
> evil heart of unbelief, in departing from the living
> God. But exhort one another daily, while it is called
> To day; lest any of you be hardened through the
> deceitfulness of sin.

This verse has nothing to do with exhorting one
another to feel the pain of being victimized or to follow
the process developed by Crabb. The exhortation is to
remain true to the faith lest one develop unbelief and
turn away from God. The "evil heart of unbelief" is not
the unconscious, but the conscious choice of unbelief and
deliberate turning away from God. The hardening does
not refer to building protective layers around the unconscious fear and pain. It is the stubbornness of unbelief.
The same chapter refers to the Israelites having hard-
ened their hearts when they were tempted in the wilder-
ness. Such a hardening is a refusal to believe and obey
God.

Crabb offers his psychological method to all Christians, because he believes that exposing the unconscious
needs, fears, pains, and wrong strategies is a necessary
means for personal Christian growth. He contends that

this is the way people become truly dependent on God. He says:

> Until we admit that nothing and no one else really satisfies, we're never going to depend on Christ. And the only way to admit that there is no real satisfaction apart from Christ is to feel the disappointment in every other relationship.[20]

For Crabb, the basis for dependence on God is our need to be respected and loved, rather than our own inability to love and obey God. And while God does indeed bless His children, dependence on God begins with the Holy Spirit revealing our own depravity, not with our own disappointments and victimization by others.

In attempting to bring people to dependence on God through making miserable mountains out of past disappointments and by focusing on feelings of being victimized, dependence can easily shift from God to a more temporal source of help, that is, the process itself. And it appears to be an endless one, for one can never rid himself of sin by recalling past hurts and disappointments and feeling them to the uttermost. It's like an endless wheel with group members taking turns. It seems as though God's truth, grace, peace, and joy are replaced by confusion, works, probing and pain. Nevertheless, Crabb says that if Christians are to be genuine and inspire others to desire what they have, they must go through that kind of processing.[21]

Crabb proposes "an approach that equips us to dive into the cesspool of the human heart . . ." which "requires that we face the fallen structure in all of its loathsome, stubborn, wicked power and submit to a painful process of dismantling."[22] Crabb contends that this fallen structure has a foundation of doubting God's goodness.[23] He says that "we must face up to how bad we hurt, how deeply we long for someone to relieve that hurt, and how poorly we trust God to look after our interests."[24] That is part of Crabb's method even though he immediately says:

> Next, we must give up any hope of finding a method that will allow us to trust God better. We must simply do our best to obey, to pray, and to soak in his Word, and then, when months, perhaps years, pass by without any visible change in our experience of him or our dealings with others, we will be introduced to **deeper capacities** within us for passionate trust.[25] (Bold added.)

Where is Crabb looking for the "deeper capacities within us"? Are these there in the natural man or are the "deeper capacities within us for passionate trust" found in Christ in us? Crabb is often unclear about the nature of one who has been born again. As he seeks to describe the nature of people, he often fails to make a clear distinction between the "old man, which is corrupt according to deceitful lusts," and the "new man, which after God is created in righteousness and true holiness." His psychological understanding of man is made up of human opinions about the old man. His means of finding God is to discover both the "cesspool" of depravity and "deeper capacities within us for passionate trust." Thus Crabb's means of finding God is to look inside ourselves in addition to reading and obeying the Word and praying.

While he says there's no method to finding God, Crabb leads his readers up five floors from what he calls the "Foundation" of "the Fallen Structure of the Human Personality." He labels his "Foundation" as "I DOUBT GOD." The subsequent floors one must go through are "First Floor: I NEED YOU"; "Second Floor: I HATE YOU"; "Third

Floor: I HATE ME"; "Fourth Floor: BUT I WILL SURVIVE";
"Fifth Floor: HERE'S HOW!"[26] These definitely reflect a
psychological perspective. Crabb hopes to move people
over to another foundation titled "I BELIEVE GOD."[27] Each
floor is the opposite of the other five floors. However, the
way to move from one foundation and through the five
floors of what he calls "The Godly Structure" is an amalgamation of psychology and the Bible.

Crabb thus describes the natural man according to a
psychological viewpoint and then attempts to move the
person to finding God through an amalgamation of
psychology and the Bible. Of stellar importance in
Crabb's method of finding God is looking inside the self
and the damage wrought by other people and circumstances. In other words, the hidden pain of past hurts and
disappointments must still be exposed and experienced at
the conscious level. Crabb says:

> We will glimpse God when our fallen structure is
> undermined and we are enticed to pursue God as
> the final good in our lives. For that to occur, we must
> have the courage to do three things.
> First, we must *face our impact on people.* . . .
> Second, we must *face the damage done to us by
> other people.* . . .
> Third, we must *face our attitude toward God.* . . .[28]

But then, as has been typical through the years,
Crabb is careful to warn his readers: "Spending more
time in Bible study and dropping to our knees more
frequently in prayer sometimes helps us avoid the very
realities of life that, if faced, could meaningfully drive us
to God."[29]

Crabb's Theory of Sanctification

Crabb's doctrine of change involves exposing unconscious pain and changing unconscious strategies. As such, his doctrine of sanctification requires one to alter his unconscious beliefs and strategies about how to satisfy his deepest needs/longings. Again, as with the other psychological doctrines that uphold this model of counseling, one cannot find any orthodox theologian throughout church history who interprets the biblical doctrine of sanctification in such a manner.

Crabb's doctrine of sanctification is not based on either an orthodox understanding of Scripture or a careful study of such key sanctification passages as Romans 6-8; Ephesians 4-6; 2 Corinthians 3; and Galatians 5. Nevertheless Crabb proposes that his method should influence how one approaches the Bible. He says, "*We must come to the Bible with the purpose of self-exposure consciously in mind.*"[30] (Italics his.) This technique of self-exposure with its underlying psychology is intended to perform the very work which the Lord has assigned to the Holy Spirit and the Word itself.

The Bible does more than simply set forth principles. It is activated in our lives by the Lord Himself. Psalm 19 clearly outlines what the Word of God can do:

> The law of the Lord is perfect, converting the soul; the testimony of the Lord is sure, making wise the simple.
> The statutes of the Lord are right, rejoicing the heart; the commandment of the Lord is pure, enlightening the eyes.

> The fear of the Lord is clean, enduring for ever; the judgments of the Lord are true and righteous altogether.
>
> More to be desired are they than gold, yea, than much fine gold; sweeter also than honey and the honeycomb.
>
> Moreover by them is thy servant warned; and in keeping of them there is great reward.
>
> Who can understand his errors? cleanse thou me from secret faults.
>
> Keep back thy servant also from presumptuous sins; let them not have dominion over me; then shall I be upright, and I shall be innocent from the great transgression.
>
> Let the words of my mouth, and the meditation of my heart, be acceptable in thy sight, O Lord, my strength, and my redeemer. (Psalm 19:7-14.)

This Psalm says that the Word works deep change in a person. However, it is important to remember that the Word cannot be separated from the One who spoke the Word. Whenever the Word operates in a person's life, it is the Lord working through His Word. The Lord converts the soul through His Word. The Lord cleanses from sin and makes a person pure. The Lord enlightens the eyes through His Word, enables a person to understand his errors, and cleanses that person from secret faults. The direct involvement of the Lord in the ministry of the Word is further emphasized at the end of the Psalm when David prays that the Lord will enable him to think, say, and do what is right.

While Crabb may speak of the Holy Spirit's role in the process of change, he downplays the unique work of the Holy Spirit's activities in the heart of a person who is earnestly reading the Word of God for the purpose of sanctification and obedience. He says,

> It's wrong to handle a text like an authorized Ouija board. We are not to read a passage and expect the Spirit of God to mystically impress on our conscious-ness whatever self-knowledge He wants us to have.[31]

Expecting God to speak through His Word is not the same as handling the Bible like a Ouija board. To suggest that such expectations of God directly using His Word through the ministry of the Holy Spirit is like using a Ouija board is a denial of 2 Timothy 3:16-17 as well as being contrary to the plain biblical teaching on the work of the Holy Spirit.

Crabb apparently does not trust the Holy Spirit to cause believers to develop a true passion for God without his kind of exposure. While he says that "True passion for our Lord is a work of the Holy Spirit,"[32] he also contends that "Part of our job then, if we are to find God, is to look honestly at those disturbing realities about ourselves and life—realities that could destroy all our joy unless God gives us hope."[33] It is one thing to leave all this exposure to the Lord and His Word. It is quite another thing to attempt to understand the self through integrating psychological theories to understand the self and to bring about change. There are also some differences as to what is to be exposed, the so-called powerful hidden material in a Freudian-type of unconscious that drives behavior or the sin that a person has avoided facing and confessing. Crabb has so cleverly integrated his psychological theo-ries with the Scripture that one may be thoroughly deceived about himself and the spiritual progress he may be making through Crabb's explanations and psychological processing.

Crabb presents a view of sanctification that differs radically from the historic position of the church. It represents a psychospiritual doctrine. The same theories about needs and the unconscious can be found in psychology texts. The only difference is that Crabb has added the framework of biblical references, categories, and biblical-sounding language to his psychological doctrine, which of course makes him an integrationist.

Is it possible that secular psychologists and psychiatrists who spurned God could ever have produced an interpretation of man's innermost nature and the method of change which stands in full accord with the Scriptures? It would be difficult to square such an idea with I Corinthians 1:18-2:14:

> For after that in the wisdom of God the world by wisdom knew not God, it pleased God by the foolishness of preaching to save them that believe . . . . For I determined not to know any thing among you, save Jesus Christ, and him crucified. . . . And my speech and my preaching was not with enticing words of man's wisdom, but in demonstration of the Spirit and of power; that your faith should not stand in the wisdom of men, but in the power of God. . . . **But the natural man receiveth not the things of the Spirit of God: for they are foolishness unto him: neither can he know them, because they are spiritually discerned**. (1 Cor. 1:21 and 2:2, 4, 5, 14.)

Crabb's doctrine of change falls significantly short of the doctrine of sanctification described in the New Testament. Crabb's addition of psychological speculations do not reflect the richness, fullness, and accuracy of biblical teaching on sanctification and change. Moreover, God has been successfully saving, sanctifying, and changing people throughout the centuries without the help of psychotherapy and its underlying psychologies. Adding secular, man-made psychological ideas and methods of change to the Word of God and the work of the Holy Spirit regarding sanctification is preaching another gospel by adding additional means and requirements.

Notes

Larry Crabb's Gospel
1. Lawrence J. Crabb, Jr., *Understanding People* (Grand Rapids: Zondervan Publishing House, 1987), p. 211.

Chapter 1: Has Larry Crabb Changed?
1. Larry Crabb, Letter to the Editor, *Christianity Today* (October 2, 1995), p. 8.
2. Larry Crabb, *Connecting* (Nashville: Word Publishing, 1997), p. 11.
3. *Ibid.*, p. 11.
4. Lawrence J. Crabb, Jr., *Basic Principles of Biblical Counseling* (Grand Rapids: Zondervan Publishing House, 1975).
5. Lawrence J. Crabb, Jr., *Effective Biblical Counseling* (Grand Rapids: Zondervan Publishing House, 1977).
6. Crabb, *Basic Principles of Biblical Counseling, op. cit.*, jacket cover.
7. Lawrence J. Crabb, Jr., "Moving the Couch into the Church," *Christianity Today* (Sept. 22, 1978), p. 17.
8. *Ibid.*, p. 18.
9. *Ibid.*
10. *Ibid.*
11. *Ibid.*
12. *Ibid.*
13. *Ibid.*
14. *Ibid.*, p. 19.
15. *Ibid.*
16. For an overview of these ungodly theories, see Martin and Deidre Bobgan, *The End of "Christian Psychology"* (Santa Barbara: EastGate Publishers, 1997).
17. Crabb, "Moving the Couch into the Church," *op. cit.*, p. 17.
18. Larry Crabb, *Finding God* (Grand Rapids, MI: Zondervan Publishing House, 1993).
19. Kevin Dale Miller, "Putting an End to Christian Psychology," *Christianity Today* (August 14, 1995), pp. 16,17.
20. Lawrence J. Crabb, Jr., "Moving the Couch into the Church," *op. cit.*, p. 18.
21. Lawrence J. Crabb, Jr., *Inside Out* (Colorado Springs: NavPress, 1988).
22. Lawrence J. Crabb, Jr., *Understanding People* (Grand Rapids: Zondervan Publishing House, 1987).
23. Crabb, "Moving the Couch into the Church," *op. cit.*, p. 19
24. Larry Crabb, Moody Bible Institute 1995 Pastors' Conference.
25. *Ibid.*
26. Crabb, *Inside Out, op. cit.*, p. 186.
27. Inside Out: A Four Part Film Series with Dr. Larry Crabb (Colorado Springs: NavPress, 1988), Film 2.
28. Larry Crabb, Moody Bible Institute 1995 Pastors' Conference.
29. *Ibid.*
30. *Ibid.*
31. Larry Crabb, *Inside Out, op. cit.*, p. 210.
32. *Ibid.*, p. 211.
33. *Ibid.*
34. Lawrence J. Crabb, Jr., *The Marriage Builder* (Grand Rapids: Zondervan Publishing House,1982).
35. Larry Crabb, Moody Bible Institute 1995 Pastors' Conference.
36. *Ibid.*
37. *Ibid.*
38. Martin and Deidre Bobgan, *The End of "Christian Psychology,"* *op. cit.*

Chapter 2: Crabb's Shifts and Expansions

1. Larry Crabb and Dan B. Allender, *Hope When You're Hurting* (Grand Rapids, MI: Zondervan Publishing House, 1996), p. 9.
2. Larry Crabb, *Connecting* (Nashville: Word Publishing, 1997), p. xii.
3. *Ibid.*, p. xx.
4. *Ibid.*, p. xvi.
5. *Ibid.*
6. *Ibid.*
7. Lawrence J. Crabb, Jr., "Moving the Couch into the Church," *Christianity Today* (Sept. 22, 1978), p. 19.
8. Crabb, *Connecting, op. cit.*, p. 175.
9. *Ibid.* p. xiii.
10. Crabb and Allender, *Hope when You're Hurting, op. cit.*, p. 187.
11. Crabb, *Connecting, op. cit.*, p. 97.
12. Larry Crabb quoted in "A Second Look at the Views of Dr. Larry Crabb, *CAPS Report*, Vol. 24, Issue 3 (Winter 1995), p. 1.
13. Crabb and Allender, *Hope when You're Hurting, op. cit.*, p. 187.
14. Lawrence J. Crabb, Jr., *Effective Biblical Counseling* (Grand Rapids: Zondervan Publishing House, 1977), p. 48.
15. Larry Crabb, *Finding God* (Grand Rapids, MI: Zondervan Publishing Company, 1993), p. 16.
16. Linda Riebel, "Theory as Self-Portrait and the Ideal of Objectivity," *Journal of Humanistic Psychology* (Spring 1982), pp. 91,92.
17. Crabb, "Moving the Couch into the Church," *op. cit.*, p. 17.
18. Crabb, *Connecting, op. cit.*, p. xviii.
19. *Ibid.*
20. *Ibid.*
21. *The Family Therapy Networker*, Vol. 21, No. 6.
22. *Ibid.*
23. Jerome Frank, "Therapeutic Factors in Psychotherapy," *American Journal of Psychotherapy*, Vol. 25 (1971), p. 360.
24. Crabb and Allender, *Hope when You're Hurting, op. cit.*, p. 179.
25. *Ibid.*
26. *Ibid.*
27. *Ibid.*
28. Crabb, *Connecting, op. cit.*, pp. 10,11.
29. *Ibid.*, p. 79.
30. *Ibid.*, p. 82.
31. *Ibid.*
32. *Ibid.*, p. 158.
33. *Ibid.*
34. *Ibid.*, p. 175.
35. *Ibid.*, p. 183.
36. *Ibid.*
37. *Ibid.*, p. 191.
38. *Ibid.*, p. 203.
39. *Ibid.*
40. *Ibid.*, p. 204.
41. *Ibid.*, p. 205.
42. *Ibid.*, p. 206.
43. *Ibid.*, p. 207.
44. Crabb quoted in "A Second Look at the Views of Dr. Larry Crabb," *op. cit.*, p. 6.
45. Larry Crabb quoted in Kevin Dale Miller, "Putting an End to Christian Psychology," *Christianity Today* (August 14, 1995), p. 17.
46. Crabb quoted in "A Second Look at the Views of Dr. Larry Crabb," *op. cit.*, p. 6.
47. Crabb and Allender, *Hope when You're Hurting, op. cit.*, p.144.

Chapter 3: Self-Disclosure, Exposure and Community

1. Carl R. Rogers, "Interpersonal Relationship: The Core of Guidance" in Carl R. Rogers and Barry Stevens, *Person to Person: The Problem of Being Human* (Lafayette, CA: Real People Press, 1967), p. 90.
2. Larry Crabb, *Finding God* (Grand Rapids, MI: Zondervan Publishing House, 1993), pp. 70,71.
3. *Ibid.*, p. 71.
4. *Ibid.*, p. 72.
5. *Ibid.*, p. 81.
6. *Ibid.*, p. 72.
7. *Ibid.*, p. 81.
8. Philip Yancey, "The Holy Inefficiency of Henri Nouwen," *Christianity Today,* Vol. 40, No. 14 (Dec. 9, 1996), p. 80.
9. Henri Nouwen, *The Inner Voice of Love: A Journey Through Anguish to Freedom* (New York: Doubleday, 1996), xiii, xiv, quoted by Larry Crabb in *Connecting* (Nashville: Word Publishing, 1997, pp. 24,25.
10. Crabb, *Connecting, op. cit.*, p. 25.
11. *Ibid.*, p. xiv.
12. M. Scott Peck, *The Different Drum: Community Making and Peace* (New York: Simon & Schuster, Inc., 1987), p. 47.
13. *Ibid.*, p. 50.
14. *Ibid.*
15. Crabb, *Connecting, op. cit.*, p. 43.
16. *Ibid.*, pp. 1-6.
17. *Ibid.*, p. 49.
18. *Ibid.*
19. *Ibid.*, p. 65.
20. *Ibid.*, p. 45.
21. *Ibid.*, p. 46.
22. *Ibid.*, p. 73.
23. *Ibid.*, p. 74.
24. *Ibid.*, p. xvi.
25. *Ibid.*
26. *Ibid.*, p. xvii.
27. *Ibid.*, p. xviii.
28. *Ibid.*, p. 32.
29. *Ibid.*, p. 29.
30. Ad for Institute for Biblical Community seminars on "Connecting," *Christianity Today*, Vol. 42, No. 5, (April 27, 1998), p. 5.
31. Crabb, *Connecting, op. cit.*, p. xviii.
32. *Ibid.*, p. xx.
33. *Ibid.*, p. 9.
34. *Ibid.*
35. *Ibid.*
36. *Ibid.*, p. 58.
37. *Ibid.*
38. *Ibid.*, p. 59.
39. *Ibid.*
40. *Ibid.*
41. *Ibid.*, p. 60.
42. *Ibid.*, p. 59.
43. *Ibid.*, p. 65.
44. *Ibid.*, p. 73.
45. *Ibid.*, p. 74.
46. *Ibid.*
47. *Ibid.*, p. 82.
48. *Ibid.*, p. 59.
49. *Ibid.*

Chapter 4: Integrating Psychology and the Bible

1. Lawrence J. Crabb, Jr., *Effective Biblical Counseling* (Grand Rapids: Zondervan Publishing House, 1977), p. 15.
2. *Ibid.*
3. Lawrence J. Crabb, Jr., *Understanding People* (Grand Rapids: Zondervan Publishing House, 1987), pp. 66-72.
4. Crabb, *Effective Biblical Counseling, op. cit.*, pp. 47-56.
5. *Ibid.*, p. 48.
6. *Ibid.*, pp. 35-46.
7. *Ibid.*, p. 52.
8. Crabb, *Understanding People, op. cit.*, pp. 66-67.
9. *Ibid.*, p. 63.
10. *Ibid.*, pp, 54, 56-57.
11. *Ibid.*, p. 56.
12. *Ibid.*, pp. 63, 70ff.
13. *Ibid.*, p. 69.
14. *Ibid.*, p. 56.
15. *Ibid.*, pp. 57-58.
16. *Ibid.*, p. 58.
17. *Ibid.*, p. 57.
18. *Ibid.*
19. *Ibid.*, pp. 55-58.
20. *Ibid.*
21. *Ibid.*, p. 58.
22. *Ibid.*, p. 57.
23. Larry Crabb, *Connecting* (Nashville: Word Publishing, 1997), p. xvii.

Chapter 5: The Use and Praise of Psychology

1. Lawrence J. Crabb, Jr., *Understanding People* (Grand Rapids: Zondervan Publishing House, 1987), p. 15.
2. Lawrence J. Crabb, Jr., *Effective Biblical Counseling* (Grand Rapids: Zondervan Publishing House, 1977), p. 52ff.
3. *Ibid.*, p. 56.
4. *Ibid.*, p. 15.
5. *Ibid.*, p. 37.
6. Lawrence J. Crabb, Jr., *Basic Principles of Biblical Counseling* (Grand Rapids: Zondervan Publishing House, 1975), p. 77.
7. Larry Crabb, *Connecting* (Nashville: Word Publishing, 1997), p 46.
8. Carl Rogers, Graduation Address, Sonoma State College, quoted in William Kirk Kilpatrick, *The Emperor's New Clothes* (Westchester, IL: Crossway Books, 1985), p. 162.
9. Crabb, *Connecting, op. cit.*, p. 46.
10. J. P. Chaplin, *Dictionary of Psychology*, Revised Edition (New York: Dell Publishing Company, 1968), pp. 555-556.
11. Crabb, *Understanding People, op. cit.*, p. 59.
12. *Ibid.*, p. 61.
13. *Ibid.*, pp. 215-216.
14. Lawrence J. Crabb, Jr., *Inside Out* (Colorado Springs: NavPress, 1988), pp. 14-15, 32, 44-49, 73, 119, 122, 128.
15. *Ibid.*, pp. 44, 52-53, 182ff.
16. Crabb, *Connecting, op. cit.*, p. 19.
17. Crabb, *Understanding People, op. cit.*, p. 142ff.
18. *Ibid.*, pp. 143-144.
19. *Ibid.*, p. 144.
20. *Ibid.*, pp. 48-58, 144ff.
21. *Ibid.*, pp. 144-145.
22. *Ibid.*, pp. 126-130.
23. *Ibid.*, p. 129.

24. *Ibid.*
25. Ernest R. Hilgard, Rita L. Atkinson, Richard C. Atkinson, *Introduction to Psychology*, 7th Edition (New York: Harcourt, Brace, Jovanovich, Inc., 1979), p. 389.
26. Jeffrey Masson, *Against Therapy* (New York: Atheneum, 1988), p. 45ff.
27. Crabb, *Inside Out, op. cit.*, pp. 44, 182.
28. Crabb, *Understanding People, op. cit.*, p. 142.
29. *Ibid.*, pp. 44, 182.
30. *Ibid.*, p. 129.
31. *Ibid.*
32. Crabb, *Effective Biblical Counseling, op. cit.*, p. 43.
33. Larry Crabb, *Finding God* (Grand Rapids, MI: Zondervan Publishing House, 1993), p. 44.
34. B. H. Shulman, "Adlerian Psychotherapy," *Encyclopedia of Psychology.* Raymond J. Corsini, ed. (New York: John Wiley and Sons, 1984), p. 18.
35. Alfred Adler, *The Practice of Individual Psychology* (New York: Harcourt, Brace & Company, Inc., 1929), p. 10.
36. *Ibid.*, p. 21.
37. Crabb, *Inside Out, op. cit.*, pp. 167-170.
38. Crabb, *Finding God, op. cit.*, p. 165.
39. Crabb, *Effective Biblical Counseling, op. cit.*, p. 152; Crabb, *Understanding People, op. cit.*, p. 203.
40. Shulman, *op. cit.*, p. 19.
41. Crabb, *Finding God, op. cit.*,.p. 45.
42. Shulman, *op. cit.*, p. 20.
43. *Ibid.*
44. H. H. Mosak, "Adlerian Psychology," *Encyclopedia of Psychology*, Raymond J. Corsini, ed. (New York: John Wiley and Sons, 1984), p. 18.
45. Albert Ellis, "Is Religiosity Pathological?" *Free Inquiry*, Spring 1988(927-32), p. 27.
46. *Ibid.*, p. 31.
47. *Ibid.*
48. Crabb, *Effective Biblical Counseling, op. cit.*, p. 56.

Chapter 6: The Unconscious: A Key to Understanding?
1. "Why Freud Isn't Dead," *Scientific American* (December 1996), p. 74.
2. Letter on file.
3. Lawrence J. Crabb, Jr., *Understanding People* (Grand Rapids: Zondervan Publishing House, 1987), pp. 126ff., 142ff.; Lawrence J. Crabb, Jr., *Effective Biblical Counseling* (Grand Rapids: Zondervan Publishing House, 1977), p. 91ff.
4. Crabb, *Effective Biblical Counseling, op. cit.*, p. 91.
5. *Ibid.*, p. 92.
6. Lawrence J. Crabb, Jr. and Dan B. Allender, *Encouragement* (Grand Rapids: Zondervan Publishing House, 1984), p. 95.
7. Crabb, *Understanding People, op. cit.*, p. 148.
8. *Ibid.*
9. Lawrence J. Crabb, Jr., *The Marriage Builder* (Grand Rapids: Zondervan Publishing House,1982), p. 49.
10. Crabb, *Understanding People, op. cit.*, p. 144.
11. *Ibid.*, pp. 144-145.
12. Karl Popper, "Scientific Theory and Falsifiability," *Perspectives in Philosophy* (Robert N. Beck, ed. New York: Holt, Rinehart, Winston, 1975), p. 343.
13. *Ibid.*, pp. 344-345.
14. *Ibid.*, p. 344.
15. *Ibid.*, p. 343.
16. Carol Tavris, "Freedom to Change," *Prime Time* (October 1980), p. 28.
17. Jerome Frank, "Therapeutic Factors in Psychotherapy," *American Journal of Psychotherapy*, Vol. 25 (1971), p. 356.
18. Crabb, *Understanding People, op. cit.*, p. 146.
19. *Ibid.*

20. *Ibid.*
21. *Ibid.*
22. Lawrence J. Crabb, Jr., *Inside Out* (Colorado Springs: NavPress, 1988), pp. 54, 64, 93.
23. *Ibid.*, pp. 44, 54, 80-81, 92, etc.
24. *Ibid.*, pp. 64.
25. *Ibid.*, p. 57.
26. Crabb, *Effective Biblical Counseling, op. cit.*, p. 91.
27. *Ibid.*, p. 91.
28. *Ibid.*, pp. 47-49.
29. W. E. Vine, *The Expanded Vine's Expository Dictionary of New Testament Words* (John Kohlenberger III, ed. Minneapolis: Bethany House Publishers, 1984), pp. 741-742.
30. Crabb, *Understanding People, op. cit.*, p. 129.
31. *Ibid.*, p. 129ff.; Crabb, *Effective Biblical Counseling, op. cit.*, p. 78; Crabb, *Basic Principles of Biblical Counseling, op, cit.*, p. 80.
32. Crabb, *Understanding People, op. cit.*, pp. 142-143.
33. Houston Smith, *The Religions of Man* (New York: Harper & Row, 1965), p. 52.
34. *Ibid.*, pp. 52-53.

Chapter 7: Need-Driven Theology

1. Lawrence J. Crabb, Jr., *Basic Principles of Biblical Counseling* (Grand Rapids: Zondervan Publishing House, 1975), p. 53.
2. Lawrence J. Crabb, Jr., *Effective Biblical Counseling* (Grand Rapids: Zondervan Publishing House, 1977), p. 61.
3. *Ibid.*, pp. 60-61.
4. *Ibid.*, pp. 91-96.
5. Lawrence J. Crabb, Jr., *Understanding People* (Grand Rapids: Zondervan Publishing House, 1987), p. 146ff.
6. Lawrence J. Crabb, Jr., *Inside Out* (Colorado Springs: NavPress, 1988), pp. 52-56.
7. Larry Crabb, *Finding God* (Grand Rapids, MI: Zondervan Publishing House, 1993), p. 16.
8. Crabb, *Inside Out. op. cit.*, p. 125.
9. *Ibid.*, p. 127.
10. Crabb, *Understanding People, op. cit.*, p. 188.
11. Crabb, *Inside Out, op. cit.*, p. 114.
12. Crabb, *Basic Principles of Biblical Counseling, op. cit.*, p. 53.
13. Lawrence J. Crabb, Jr. and Dan B. Allender, *Encouragement* (Grand Rapids: Zondervan Publishing House, 1984), pp. 31-36; Crabb, *Effective Biblical Counseling, op. cit.*, p. 61.
14. Crabb, *Effective Biblical Counseling, op. cit.*, p. 71.
15. Crabb, *Understanding People, op. cit.*, pp. 130-138.
16. *Ibid.*, p. 129.
17. *Ibid.*, pp. 148-152.
18. *Ibid.*, p. 165.
19. *Ibid.*, pp. 158-168.
20. *Ibid.*, pp. 171-189.
21. Crabb, *Understanding People, op. cit.*, p. 15.
22. Crabb, *Effective Biblical Counseling, op. cit.*, pp. 60-61.
23. Crabb, *Inside Out, op. cit.*, p. 83.
24. Lawrence J. Crabb, Jr., *The Marriage Builder* (Grand Rapids: Zondervan Publishing House, 1982), p. 29.
25. Crabb, *Effective Biblical Counseling, op. cit.*, p. 139.
26. Tony Walter, *Need: The New Religion* (Downers Grove: InterVarsity Press, 1985), Preface.
27. *Ibid.*, p. 5.
28. *Ibid.*, p. 13.
29. *Ibid.*, p. 161.

30. *Ibid.*, p. 111.
31. Crabb, *Understanding People, op. cit.*, pp. 93-96.
32. *Ibid.*, p. 93.
33. *Ibid.*, p. 15.

Chapter 8: Unconscious Motivators of Behavior
1. Lawrence J. Crabb, Jr., *Effective Biblical Counseling* (Grand Rapids: Zondervan Publishing House, 1977), p. 74ff.
2. Lawrence J. Crabb, Jr., *Understanding People* (Grand Rapids: Zondervan Publishing House, 1987), p. 93-96.
3. Lawrence J. Crabb, Jr., *Basic Principles of Biblical Counseling* (Grand Rapids: Zondervan Publishing House, 1975), p. 74; Crabb, *Effective Biblical Counseling, op. cit.*, pp. 60-61, 116, 118, etc.; Crabb, *Understanding People, op. cit.*, pp. 146-148; Lawrence J. Crabb, Jr., *Inside Out* (Colorado Springs: NavPress, 1988), p. 54.
4. Crabb, *Effective Biblical Counseling, op. cit.*, p. 76.
5. Crabb, *Understanding People, op. cit.*, p. 93ff.
6. Crabb, *Effective Biblical Counseling, op. cit.*, p. 76.
7. *Ibid.*
8. *Ibid.*
9. Crabb, *Inside Out, op. cit.*, pp. 15, 16, 18.
10. Crabb, *Effective Biblical Counseling, op. cit.*, pp. 76-77.
11. *Ibid.*, pp. 77-78.
12. *Ibid.*, p. 74ff.
13. A. H. Maslow, *Motivation and Personality* (New York:Harper & Brothers Publishers, 1954), p. 90.
14. *Ibid.*, p. 91.
15. *Ibid.*, p. 105.
16. Lawrence J. Crabb, Jr., *The Marriage Builder* (Grand Rapids: Zondervan Publishing House, 1982), p. 29.
17. *Ibid.*
18. Crabb, *Understanding People, op. cit.*, p. 134.
19. *Ibid.*, p. 109.
20. *Ibid.*
21. *Ibid.*
22. Crabb, *Inside Out, op. cit.*, p. 64.
23. Crabb, *Understanding People, op. cit.*, p. 111.
24. *Ibid.*, p. 15.
25. Crabb, *Effective Biblical Counseling, op. cit.*, p. 61.
26. Crabb, *Understanding People, op. cit.*, p. 105.
27. *Ibid.*
28. *Ibid.*, p. 106.
29. *Ibid.*, p. 105.
30. *Ibid.*
31. *Ibid.*, p. 106.
32. Crabb, *Inside Out, op. cit.*, p. 69.
33. *Ibid.*, p. 92.
34. Crabb, *Understanding People, op. cit.*, p. 105.
35. *Ibid.*, p. 107ff.
36. *Ibid.*, p. 105.
37. *Ibid.*, pp. 104-107 with 142-152.

Chapter 9: Limits of Consciousness
1. Lawrence J. Crabb, Jr., *Effective Biblical Counseling* (Grand Rapids: Zondervan Publishing House, 1977), p. 91ff.
2. *Ibid.*, pp. 91-96.
3. Lawrence J. Crabb, Jr., *Inside Out* (Colorado Springs: NavPress, 1988), pp. 52ff.
4. Lawrence J. Crabb, Jr., *Understanding People* (Grand Rapids: Zondervan Publishing House, 1987), p. 147ff.

5. Crabb, *Effective Biblical Counseling, op. cit.*, pp. 76ff., 91-96; Crabb, *Understanding People, op. cit.*, pp. 130, 146ff.; Crabb, *Inside Out, op. cit.*, pp. 44ff., 182ff.
6. Crabb, *Understanding People, op. cit.*, p. 145.
7. Crabb, *Effective Biblical Counseling, op. cit.*, p. 69.
8. Lawrence J. Crabb, Jr., *Basic Principles of Biblical Counseling* (Grand Rapids: Zondervan Publishing House, 1975), p. 87.
9. Crabb, *Effective Biblical Counseling, op. cit.*, p. 91.
10. *Ibid.*
11. *Ibid.*, p. 92.
12. Lawrence J. Crabb, Jr., *The Marriage Builder* (Grand Rapids: Zondervan Publishing House,1982), p. 48.
13. *Ibid.*
14. Crabb, *Understanding People, op. cit.*, p. 147.
15. *Ibid.*, p. 143.
16. *Ibid.*, p. 148.
17. Crabb, *Inside Out, op. cit.*, p. 54.
18. *Ibid.*, pp. 44ff., 182ff.
19. Crabb, *Basic Principles of Biblical Counseling, op. cit.*, pp. 56-57, 74; Crabb, *Effective Biblical Counseling, op. cit.*, pp. 69, 105, 116.
20. Larry Crabb, *Connecting* (Nashville: Word Publishing, 1997), p. 77.
21. Lawrence J. Crabb, Jr. and Dan B. Allender, *Encouragement* (Grand Rapids: Zondervan Publishing House, 1984),   pp. 86-89.
22. *Ibid.*, p. 87.
23. *Ibid.*
24. Crabb, *Inside Out, op. cit.*, p. 121ff.
25. Carol Tavris, *Anger: The Misunderstood Emotion* (New York: Simon and Schuster, 1982), p. 36.
26. Crabb, *Encouragement, op. cit.*, p. 33.
27. Crabb, *Understanding People, op. cit.*, p. 115.
28. *Ibid.*, p. 67.
29. *Ibid.*
30. Crabb, *Inside Out, op. cit.*, pp. 15, 16, 18.
31. *Ibid.*, p. 29.
32. *Ibid.*, p. 99.
33. Crabb, *Understanding People, op. cit.*, p. 149ff.; Crabb, *Inside Out, op. cit.*, p. 116ff.
34. Crabb, *Understanding People, op. cit.*, p. 144.
35. *Ibid.*
36. *Ibid.*
37. Crabb, *Inside Out, op. cit.*, p. 119.
38. *Ibid.*, p. 120.
39. *Ibid.*, pp. 119-120.
40. Crabb, *Understanding People, op. cit.*, pp. 149-152.
41. *Ibid.*, pp. 149-150.
42. Crabb, *Inside Out, op. cit.*, p. 184.
43. *Ibid.*
44. Crabb, *Effective Biblical Counseling, op. cit.*, p. 90.
45. *Ibid.*, pp. 91-94.
46. Crabb, *Understanding People, op. cit.*, pp. 94, 158-165.
47. *Ibid.*, p. 159.
48. Alfred Adler, *The Practice of Individual Psychology* (New York: Harcourt, Brace & Company, Inc., 1929), p. 4.
49. Crabb, *Understanding People, op. cit.*, p. 161.
50. *Ibid.*, p. 95, 188-189.

Chapter 10: The Exposing Process

1. Lawrence J. Crabb, Jr., *Understanding People* (Grand Rapids: Zondervan Publishing House, 1987), p. 144.

2. Lawrence J. Crabb, Jr., *Effective Biblical Counseling* (Grand Rapids: Zondervan Publishing House, 1977), p. 95.
3. Lawrence J. Crabb, Jr., *Inside Out* (Colorado Springs: NavPress, 1988), p. 89.
4. Crabb, *Understanding People, op. cit.*, pp. 13ff., 67ff., 101ff., 146ff.; Crabb, *Inside Out, op. cit.*, pp. 14ff., 32ff., 74ff., 90ff., 116ff., 156ff.
5. Crabb, *Effective Biblical Counseling, op. cit.*, p. 46.
6. Crabb, *Inside Out, op. cit.*, p. 170.
7. *Ibid.*, p. 167.
8. Crabb, *Effective Biblical Counseling, op. cit.*, p. 46.
9. John Rowan, "Nine Humanistic Heresies," *Journal of Humanistic Psychology*, Vol. 27, No. 2, Spring 1987 (141-157), pp. 143-144.
10. Crabb, *Understanding People, op. cit.*, p. 130.
11. Crabb, *Inside Out, op. cit.*, p. 186.
12. J. P. Chaplin, *Dictionary of Psychology*, New Revised Version (New York: Dell Publishing Co., Inc., 1968), p. 2.
13. Sol Garfield and Allen E. Bergin, eds., *Handbook of Psychotherapy and Behavior Change*, 2nd Ed. (New York: John Wiley and Sons, 1978), p. 180.
14. David A. Shapiro, "Comparative Credibility of Treatment Rationales," *British Journal of Clinical Psychology*, 1981, Vol. 20 (111-122), p. 112.
15. Crabb, *Inside Out, op. cit.*, p. 165.
16. *Ibid.*, p. 185.
17. *Ibid.*, p. 186.
18. *Ibid.*
19. *Ibid.*, p. 165.
20. Inside Out: A Four Part Film Series with Dr. Larry Crabb (Colorado Springs: NavPress, 1988), Film 2.
21. Crabb, *Inside Out, op. cit.*, p. 64.
22. Larry Crabb, *Finding God* (Grand Rapids, MI: Zondervan Publishing House, 1993), p. 81.
23. *Ibid.*, p. 87.
24. *Ibid.*, p. 115.
25. *Ibid.*
26. *Ibid.*, p. 148.
27. *Ibid.*, p. 149
28. *Ibid.*, pp. 158,159.
29. *Ibid.*, p. 161.
30. Crabb, *Inside Out, op. cit.*, p. 163.
31. *Ibid.*, p. 161.
32. Crabb, *Finding God, op. cit.*, p. 53.
33. *Ibid.*, p. 54.

For a sample copy of a free newsletter about the intrusion of psychological counseling theories and therapies into Christianity, please write to:

PsychoHeresy Awareness Ministries
4137 Primavera Road
Santa Barbara, CA 93110

phone: 1-800-216-4696

e-mail: bobgan@psychoheresy-aware.org

Web Site Address:

www.psychoheresy-aware.org

Also available from this ministry:
Three position papers regarding Larry Crabb's teachings:

1. "Inside and Back Out with Dr. Larry Crabb" by Jim Owen

2. "Recovery or the Bible or . . . Crabb's 'Third' Way"? by Debbie Dewart

3. "Trevor Morrison: Devoted to God and His Word or to Dr. Lawrence Crabb and His Teachings?" by Martin & Deidre Bobgan

For information, contact
PsychoHeresy Awareness Ministries

OTHER BOOKS FROM EASTGATE

The End of "Christian Psychology" by Martin and Deidre Bobgan discusses research about the question,"Does psychotherapy work?" analyzes why Christians use psychological counseling, and gives evidence showing that professional psychotherapy with its underlying psychologies is questionable at best, detrimental at worst, and a spiritual counterfeit at least. The book includes descriptions and analyses of major psychological theorists and reveals that "Christian psychology" involves the same problems and confusions of contradictory theories and techniques as secular psychology. This book presents enough biblical and scientific evidence to shut down both secular and "Christian psychology."

PsychoHeresy: The Psychological Seduction of Christianity by Martin and Deidre Bobgan exposes the fallacies and failures of psychological counseling theories and therapies for one purpose: to call the Church back to curing souls by means of the Word of God and the work of the Holy Spirit rather than by man-made means and opinions. Besides revealing the anti-Christian biases, internal contradictions, and documented failures of secular psychotherapy, *PsychoHeresy* examines various amalgamations of secular psychologies with Christianity and explodes firmly entrenched myths that undergird those unholy unions.

12 Steps to Destruction: Codependency/Recovery Heresies by the Bobgans provides information for Christians about codependency/recovery teachings, Alcoholics Anonymous, Twelve-Step groups, and addiction treatment programs. All are examined from a biblical, historical, and research perspective. The book urges believers to trust the sufficiency of Christ and the Word of God instead of Twelve-Step and codependency/recovery theories and therapies.